D0102393

One of the mills strung out along the stream at Cheesden Lumb, Lancashire.

Other books by Anthony Burton

A Programmed Guide to Office Warfare
The Jones Report
The Canal Builders
The Reluctant Musketeer
Canals in Colour
Remains of a Revolution
The Master Idol
Josiah Wedgwood
Canal (with Derek Pratt)
The Navigators
The Miners
Back Door Britain
Industrial Archaeological Sites of Britain
A Place to Stand
The Green Bag Travellers (with Pip Burton)
The Past At Work
The Rainhill Story
The Past Afloat
The Changing River
The Shell Book of Curious Britain
Our Industrial Past
The Waterways of Britain
The Rise and Fall of King Cotton
Walking the Line
Wilderness Britain
Britain's Light Railways (with John Morgan)
The Shell Book of Undiscovered Britain

Landscape Detective

The original Newbold tunnel of the Oxford Canal.

GUILD PUBLISHING, LONDON

This edition published 1986 by Book Club Associates
by arrangement with George Allen & Unwin

Allen & Unwin (Publishers) Ltd
40 Museum Street
London WC1A 1LU, UK

Allen & Unwin (Publishers) Ltd
Park Lane
Hemel Hempstead
Herts HP2 4TE, UK

Allen & Unwin Australia Pty Ltd
8 Napier Street
North Sydney, NSW 2060
Australia

Allen & Unwin with the
Port Nicholson Press
PO Box 11-838, Wellington, New Zealand

British Library Cataloguing in Publication Data

Burton, Anthony
The landscape detective.
1. Great Britain – Description and travel
I. Title II. May, John
911′.41 DA600
ISBN 0–04–914061–2

Set in 11 on 13 point Garamond by Nene Phototypesetters Ltd, Northampton,
and printed by William Clowes Limited, Beccles and London

Contents

THE INQUIRING EYE

In tradition, the role of the detective is simple. He visits the scene of the crime, carefully inspecting the ground for clues which will enable him to reconstruct the events of the past. It is a process based on observation followed by deduction. In fiction, at least, there is no end to what might be discovered by the trained observer. In *The Return of Sherlock Holmes*, a visitor bursts in on the great detective, announcing himself as John Hector McFarlane. Holmes, after a quick glance, responds: 'You mentioned your name, as if I should recognise it, but I assure you that, beyond the obvious fact that you are a bachelor, a solicitor, a Freemason, and an asthmatic, I know nothing whatever about you.' The author, perhaps wisely, leaves the reader uninformed about the chain of

The apparently unspoilt landscape of Skye. In fact even this distant view shows the dark patches of peat cutting.

logic that led from observation to deduction but, as Holmes so often remarked to Dr Watson, we know his methods. The landscape detective is not concerned with crime unless like Gibbon we think of history as 'little more than the register of the crimes, follies and misfortunes of mankind'. But he is concerned with the reconstruction of the past from observation. The evidence may be a pattern of buildings rather than a pile of cigar ash, but the method is essentially the same. And, as in the world of detective fiction, the field is open to amateurs as well as professionals. This is a book for the amateur.

The idea that the landscape itself might yield clues to the course of past events is not new; it forms the whole basis of archaeological studies. Such studies, however, rely on the infinitely slow sifting of material thrown up in carefully planned excavations and, in general, archaeology is thought of as a means of discovering aspects of history too ancient to be covered by written records. The notion that the landscape – all landscape, every bit of the land – is a record of man's work from the earliest times right through to the present day is of rather more recent origin. It is, however, a wonderfully exciting idea. It means we no longer have to worry about which places are 'historic' and which are not, for everywhere has some story to tell if only we can decipher the clues. If this all sounds a little far-fetched, then that is partly because we have become accustomed to think of history in terms of great events: battles and wars, the rise and fall of kings and parliaments. Not much of that sort of history will appear on these pages. Instead, we shall be far more concerned with the marks left behind by ordinary men and women going about their everyday business. You may go to Bosworth Field where the dynastic history of Britain was changed, where men fought under the banners of Richard III of York or of Henry Tudor. But there are no hoof marks left by the knights' chargers, no bloodstains on the grass, no crown caught up in a thorn bush. But walk through the surrounding fields and you can see the imprints left by some anonymous farmer who, year in, year out, ploughed his furrows, probably quite unaware of the greater movements of history. Landscape detectives will find themselves far more involved with the story of the peasant farmer than with that of the warring lords. The major part of this book is given over to what one might call a series of case histories, where we invite the reader to join us on a series of walks on which we shall look at the available evidence and try to draw conclusions. But before setting out on the trail it is necessary to have at least some notion of the sort of material that might come our way and what it might indicate. This introduction is not intended as a complete picture; it is rather more of a sketch, a broad outline which could be filled in with details observed on the walks.

The starting-point for any landscape study is the map, for it is only through the map that we can perceive the broad patterns on the land, unless of course we are fortunate enough to own our own helicopter. But most of us keep our feet, or at least wheels, on the ground. Now, there is no better way of observing details than by walking and looking; cars, and even bicycles, simply go too fast. What the walker does not get, however, is an overall view; he will not see, for example, the relationship of a town to its surrounding villages. But it is all there on the map and different scales of map present different pictures. Take a large sheet covering the whole of Great Britain and you can see, in a very general way, how man has established himself on the land. Here are the big cities, the towns, the villages; the crowded Midlands, the deserted Highlands. Change to a larger scale and you begin to get quite different types of information – information more closely related to direct observation. For most of the work done for this book, the standard 1:50000 Ordnance Survey maps were used. Paradoxically, you can get far more information out of this type of map than you can from one covering the whole country. And, as the father of all landscape studies, Professor W. G. Hoskins, wrote in his classic work *The Making of the English Landscape*, 'one could indeed write a whole chapter about a single sheet of the 2½-inch map, covering only six miles each way'. Certainly any 1:50000 map provides enough clues to past history to set off a lifetime of investigation. So let us look at one map and, as both authors live in Abingdon, we have selfishly chosen sheet number 164, where our home town sits at the bottom, southerly, end of the map.

The first thing to notice is the land itself and its natural features, for the land was here long before man. The most obvious features are the rivers threading the map: the Ray, the Cherwell, the Glyme, the Evenlode, the Windrush and the Thame – all eventually swelling the waters of the principal river of the region, the Thames. At the most important meeting-place of the waters, at the centre of the map, sits the one major city of the area, Oxford. It can hardly be imagined that the siting of Oxford at such a place was a mere coincidence. We shall be looking at the rivers again in more detail a little later, but another aspect of the river's influence also becomes quickly apparent. There are large areas quite devoid of those salmon-pink blotches that indicate settlements, and they are areas which, on the map, are uncut by contour lines. These are the regions of low-lying land beside the river, areas subject to flooding, wetlands. The Thames valley above Oxford is such an area, but the most obvious 'hole' in the map is the large patch to the north-east of Oxford, Otmoor, by the River Ray. The whole area is ringed by a contour line, indicating the rising ground that contains it. There are settlements in plenty in the surroundings, but on the moor itself only the ruler-straight blue lines that can only be artificial waterways suggest attempts to drain and use the moor. Already our first glance is beginning to suggest something of man's relationship to this environment.

The next most obvious physical features are the hills, some of which rise steeply from the surrounding plain. Such an area of high ground can be seen almost to surround Oxford, and another more dramatic area can be seen to the east, where Brill Hill shoots

An Oxfordshire landscape: looking down from the old track on Beckley Hill to the flat lands of Otmoor, with its straight ruled hedges that mark nineteenth-century enclosures.

up from the valley, to be crowned by a hilltop village. In the north-western corner of the map, there is a general rise in the land level towards the Cotswolds. There are also large areas of woodland spread over much of the region, and in many of these green areas you can see portions marked off in grey to indicate parkland. Again a natural feature shows special signs of adaptation by man. Other maps of other regions will show quite different physical features, but a similar process of looking and reasoning will enable the same sort of information to be deduced. What the 1:50 000 maps do not show, however, is the underlying structure, which has had a tremendous effect on man's use of the land, and it is worth turning for a moment to a geological map of the same area.

The geological map shows a series of broad stripes running roughly south-west to north-east, each stripe representing a different rock formation beneath the surface. They range from limestone in the north-west through clays and gravels to chalk in the south-east. Now, this leads to certain expectations of what we might find in travelling through the area. Until recently, man relied to a large extent on locally available material for his buildings. So, in the stone belts, we would expect to find extensive use of stone; in the clays, we would expect bricks or, in older buildings, wooden frames filled in with whatever material was most readily available. There will, however, be exceptions, for it has always been thought proper to use stone for the most important buildings, even if the stone had to be brought a considerable distance. This is no new phenomenon. Further to the south is the most remarkable prehistoric structure in the country – Stonehenge. Most of the stones were dragged many miles from the Marlborough Downs, but others were brought from much farther afield, from the Prescelly Hills of South Wales. It is conjectured that they were brought most of the way by water, going round the coast and then being brought inland by river. The significance of Stonehenge must be largely a matter of theory and supposition, though by far the likeliest explanation is that it has a religious significance, and the stones themselves, strong and durable, were necessary expressions of the durability of belief. The same feeling has carried over to more modern times, and villages and towns in the clay belt have used imported stone to build the parish church.

We are beginning, inevitably, to start to people our map with memories of the past, so it is perhaps time to turn away from the 'pure' landscape to look at man and his works. What are the earliest signs of man's presence in the area? Major sites of archaeological

The ancient and mysterious stone circle at Rollright.

interest are indicated in the OS maps in Gothic script, and many of them are shown on our sheet 164. Yet, although there is no shortage of ancient remains, they are oddly unsatisfactory, in that they seem not to bring us any closer to an understanding of the life of those times. Some of the oldest remains can be quite spectacular, such as the Hoar Stone burial chamber near Enstone (SP 377236).* What we see today are massive stones outlining what was once a chamber, a long barrow where neolithic man entombed his dead. We can see that this was an important part of the ancient settlement, for it has survived where all else has crumbled into ruin. Yet it is hard for us to form any conception of the ceremonies and beliefs that surrounded this form of burial. We can look at the collapsed stones and wonder at the effort that went into the construction of the barrow, but that brings us no closer to an understanding of the culture of that distant age. Much the same could be said of many of the ancient sites in the area. In fact, the most impressive of all these old burial sites lies just beyond the north-west corner of our map – the group known as the Rollright Stones.

* See page 197 for a note on map references.

The stones are especially interesting for they lie beside a ridge which has formed a dry route through the area since long before written records. They have, therefore, been accessible for a very long time. This is a complex site, consisting of the stone circle of rough stones, known as the King's Men; a single standing stone, the King Stone; and a group of stones leaning together as though sharing a secret, the Whispering Knights. The stones are no more comprehensible to us today than any of the great stone circles, from Stonehenge down. The Whispering Knights, however, appear to be part of a long-decayed barrow. We cannot come close to a true understanding of these stony patterns on the land. Inevitably, when facts are so difficult to come by, legend has supplied an explanation. The story has it that a king accompanied by his knights and men was met at this spot by a witch, who enticed him with dreams of glory:

Seven long strides thou shalt take,
And if Long Compton thou can see,
King of England thou shalt be.

The king, who should have known better than to trust witches, took the prophecy at face value, strode out and found the view blocked by a long barrow. The witch then claimed her triumph.

As Long Compton thou canst not see,
King of England thou shalt not be,
Rise up stick, and stand still stone,
For king of England thou shalt be none.

Thou and thy men hoar stones shall be,
And I myself an elder tree.

And there, petrified, they stand – king, knights and soldiers. It is an appealing story, but one which offers little enlightenment about the past. The stones date from the Bronze Age, more recent than the Hoar Stone, but the mystery remains impenetrable. We still know nothing of the way of life, the ordinary everyday existence of these people. Other parts of the country have different stories to tell.

Oxfordshire lacks obvious signs of the earliest ancient settlements. This is not too surprising for it is a populous area, where the past is often hidden beneath the accumulated layers of later development. Diligent searches may uncover these layers, but the evidence is neither to be seen on the map nor, in the majority of cases, on the ground. But if we turn to the wilder parts of Britain a very different picture can be seen. A lonely, bleak moor might seem to us to offer few inducements to settle down and call it home, but to another age it might have seemed an ideal site. The very poverty and thinness of the soil which inhibits growth and makes such an area unattractive to a modern agriculturist would also mean that, in an earlier age, vegetation would have been sparse and poorly developed, compared with the far denser forests of the lowlands. So it would be much easier to clear, a great advantage if your best tools are simple stone axes. And the upland site can keep you clear of danger, not least from attacks by your fellow men. So it is that when we want evidence of the life of the distant past we must turn away from the gentle lowlands and head for the moors and the hills.

The West Country provides an absolute wealth of evidence about early settlement. Look at a map of Bodmin Moor, Dartmoor or Exmoor and you will find it liberally dotted with indications of hut circles. What do these marks reveal on the ground? One of the best examples of these early settlements is to be found at Grimspound on Dartmoor (SX 701809). Here you can see a great circular stone wall, about nine feet thick – we can only guess at its original height – enclosing an area of some four acres. Within that huge circle are remains of round, stone huts; at least two dozen can be discovered by prodding about among the bracken. This is at once recognizable as a village, the houses set safely behind the defensive wall. It was in fact built around the end of the Bronze Age, some three thousand years ago.

The message of Grimspound is worth pondering, for what it tells us is that even so long ago the inhabitants of these islands had organized themselves. There was a definite social structure. People lived in individual houses, but those houses were grouped together for mutual help and protection, and the inhabitants must have collaborated in the work of building the great outer wall. What the site does not tell us is a great deal about the life of the family, of the business of living from day to day. We tend to look back at the past and see its inhabitants as some kind of alien creatures, with different needs and different desires from our own. One of the great joys of seeing the physical remains of the past lies in finding that this is not so: our ancestors were not that different after all.

Of all the ancient sites in Britain, there is none that seems to speak more directly about the distant past than Skara Brae in Orkney. There was a neolithic settlement here, but then somewhere around 1500 BC disaster struck. A great wind blew off the sea, waves crashed over the little village and when the wind died and the waves retreated the houses were left buried beneath the sand. There they remained until 1850 when another powerful storm hit the island, but this time instead of blowing sand on to the land it blew it away, and Skara Brae was brought back into the light. The houses were still there, solidly built circular huts of drystone walling, with domed roofs, the gaps between the stones blocked with clay. These are sound structures, well able to withstand the northern winter. Most remarkably, the details of the houses are also preserved. Stone slabs were set on end to form a box bed that could be filled with bracken; there is a central hearth for cooking and even what can only be described as Stone Age furniture in the shape of cupboards and dressers. It was, and is, a truly remarkable site.

Not unlike a Stone Age house in a popular cartoon, this house at Skara Brae on Orkney has stone furniture.

Our chosen area cannot offer anything to compare with these intimate domestic details of life led over three thousand years ago, but there are nonetheless important sites which show us something of the organization of the land in prehistory. The most spectacular remains are undoubtedly the hill forts, and among the finest to be found anywhere in Britain is that on Sinodun Hill across the Thames from Dorchester. The hills themselves, also known as the Wittenham Clumps, are among the best known landmarks of the Thames valley, shapely cones crowned with trees. It is only when you get closer that you see the use man has made of them. A deep ditch has been dug around the top of one of the hills, and the excavated earth and stone has been piled up to create a rampart. Within these fortifications is an enclosed area of some ten acres, and from their fort men of the Iron Age commanded views over all the surrounding country. They could look out, too, across the river to another fort built in a different style. Here the River Thame joins the Thames and the two rivers provide protection against attack. The peninsula was further guarded by a pair of banks and ditches, closing off an area of over a hundred acres. This is a promontory fort and archaeologists have located signs of circular huts and square buildings where the men and women of Dyke Hills lived and worked. From behind their defences our Iron Age ancestors would have watched the arrival of a foreign army. The Romans came here and established their own settlement, which developed over the centuries into the present town of Dorchester.

The observer on the ground gets little hint of the Roman presence at Dorchester, but the two forts – the hill fort of Sinodun and the promontory fort by the river – are still plain to see. It is not difficult to see why a conquering army should wish to impose its presence on such a well defended, strategic spot. As with prehistoric settlements, our map has little to say about a major Roman presence. Happily, other parts of the country have considerably more to tell us. Many of our cities, such as London and York, are built on Roman foundations, but the pattern of Roman building can often be seen more clearly in smaller towns. An excellent example, quite near to our area, is Cirencester. The large Roman town appears as a well organized structure, constructed on a regular grid – though there are enough variations to ensure that a study of Roman towns is of continuing interest. It would be disappointingly dreary if there was just one set pattern that was followed invariably.

The evidence derived from the landscape of prehistory helps to

The banks and ditch of Dyke Hills fort.

make sense of later events. Simply by casting our eyes over the map and taking the most casual glance at a few sites, we have already become aware of the continuity of history, of a pattern of endless change. We have not even begun to look at any kind of detail on the ground which might provide still more hints and clues, though we shall be doing just that when we come to the twelve walks. For the moment, however, let us return to our map and look at some more patterns of development. What does the map tell us about where communities have grown and, what is really a far more interesting question, why they have grown?

Look at the map, and there is not much doubt about where you should begin if you are thinking of starting with the most important centre of population. It has to be Oxford. This is one of those select places which appear in all the tourist literature as 'historic cities', occasionally even as 'ancient cities'. Oxford has certainly been around a long time, but when we think of the historic scale that contains stone circles, hill forts and Roman camps it is a comparative newcomer in the Oxfordshire landscape. To understand Oxford's origins, you have to think of England not as a stable country which for centuries has been spared foreign invasion, but as one subjected to repeated raids from continental Europe. The English, the Anglo-Saxons, represented just one element of a very important group of invaders and settlers and they in their turn were threatened by the Danes. King Alfred's great victory over the Vikings in 878 ensured the Saxon succession, but still the Viking threat remained. A series of defensive strongholds was established, all listed in a quite remarkable document, the Burghal Hidage – remarkable in that it provides so much information about these new forts that were to form the nuclei around which so many of our towns have grown. The idea was to establish a series of forts all around the borders of Wessex, into which families could retreat and which could be defended. Everything was nicely calculated. The unit of land at that time was the hide, roughly defined as the area that could be cultivated by one plough in one year. The size of the forts, or burhs, was to be determined by the number of hides they were to protect, hence the Burghal Hidage. Each fort was to have a set number of men from each hide, so that they could provide four men to defend each five yards of wall.

Turn back again to the map or, better still, look at a town map of Oxford and a pattern can be seen emerging. The city today has a curious shape, determined by the rivers Thames and Cherwell: one great block appears to the east of the Cherwell, while a second block, long and thin, spreads northwards, squeezed between the two rivers. We would expect to find considerable change and expansion in a period of over a thousand years, and if we want to find the original heart of a settlement we should look at the most obvious defensible site – the confluence of the two rivers. And there, sure enough, as clear as can be, is a regular grid pattern of streets contained within a roughly rectangular area. We have found the nucleus of our city, though we must be wary of jumping to conclusions. Even the basic pattern is not quite what it seems, for time has wrought its changes and the defences have been altered over the centuries. Roughly, however, we see a town surrounded by just over a mile of walls, with streets laid out on a regular grid, the two main roads crossing then, as they do now, at Carfax. Those who would like a much clearer notion of a Saxon burh should travel downstream from Oxford to a town which just nudges on to our map, Wallingford. Here the pattern is far less cluttered, with a rectangular defensive wall of earthworks right round the town and spreading across the river to protect the crossing-point. As the 'ford' element in both Oxford and Wallingford suggests, it was the importance of river crossings that dictated the choice of both sites.

What does this mean to the visitor to Oxford today? The answer has to be not a great deal, though parts of the old wall are still to be seen. Later developments have left more obvious marks on the town. After the Norman invasion of England, the conquerors were quick to take over the old burhs and strengthen their defences. Oxford was one of many such towns to feel the effects of the new rule: a new castle was built of the type known as motte and bailey. A mound of earth was built up to be topped by the stronghold, below which was an area contained within the outer wall, the bailey. Walk down Castle Street – and what a help street names can be in providing clues to former use – and you can still see the great motte rising up above the road. The bailey itself contained within its walls a chapel which was a collegiate church for scholars. From this small beginning, the system developed which was to make the name of Oxford synonymous with learning: the university of colleges.

Any one of dozens of guidebooks will lead you on a walk round the colleges of Oxford which, from medieval times onwards, dominated the life of the city. But to see the city purely in these terms is to misunderstand at least a part of its importance. Cities grow and develop, and change in the course of that development. Oxford long remained an essentially medieval town contained within set boundaries, though the area outside the old walls achieved a lively occupation all its own. The broad street of St Giles was home to a market and a fair – and the latter still exists, though now it is devoted to fun and games rather than the serious business of buying and selling, hiring and firing. The fair no longer has any vital role to play in the working life of Oxford.

Changed times have brought their own changes to old customs. In more recent times, the city has experienced a period of rapid growth, with whole new areas of development appearing. North Oxford developed as two quite distinct segments: the middle-class, residential area spreading up the main roads and, in the north-west, a region of close-packed streets of terraced houses, Jericho. Industry was established in the city when motor car manufacture appeared. The Morris works rapidly outgrew their modest city-centre site, and a new development was begun in Cowley to the south-east. The intervening land was soon filled in by housing, which spread outwards to absorb such old village centres as Headington. There are still plenty of gaps in the area enclosed by the modern ring road system, notably the expanse of wetland near the river, Port Meadow. This was originally left untouched because of flooding problems and is now jealously guarded as a valuable amenity, an open common within the city limits where ancient rights such as grazing are still enforced, even if today the grazing is mainly for horses and ponies kept for fun rather than livestock reared for food.

Oxford has changed, yet within the wide division there are still general patterns of another sort to be seen. When discussing the importance of the underlying geology we mentioned its effect on buildings. You can see it here in good measure. The oldest town buildings can be divided between the grand colleges and the simpler structures of everyday life. The former were, until recently, all given the dignity of stone, richly carved and pronouncing in a loud voice the importance of the institution. Elsewhere you can still find the more ordinary buildings, constructed on a timber frame. There are not many, for most have given way to later development; but you can see examples in an old shop in Cornmarket and, even more surprisingly, in the thatched pub, the Turf, tucked away behind Holywell Street. Later town-centre developers preferred stone in the form of ashlar, dressed stone presenting a smooth, urbane face to the world. Then, in Victorian times, builders turned to brick. In Jericho, this appears as diaper work, cottage fronts presenting a chequerboard effect, created by the use of alternating light and dark bricks. North Oxford is a land of brick villas, some of which are really quite grand. So, within the broad framework of the city, there is a multitude of stories to track down. And what is true of Oxford is true of virtually any town of comparable size. Each town, however, will have its own quite different set of stories to be uncovered. And if we take out our Ordnance Survey map again and look at the other towns of the region we can soon begin to see different patterns and different histories.

Bicester, Chipping Norton, Witney and Abingdon appear to be the principal centres, though a glance at the map might suggest Kidlington as another contender. We shall be looking at Abingdon in detail as a town walk (see page 167) so for the moment let us concentrate on the others, starting with Kidlington. Here the story is not quite what we might expect for this is still, officially, a village – the largest in the country. It was, in fact, quite a small place until very recently, but it lay between two major trunk roads and new housing spread out along the Banbury Road in what is a very familiar twentieth-century pattern of ribbon development. The years since the Second World War have seen an even greater increase in building, with more and more housing estates added. The old centre is still there, based on the church at the northern edge of the present village, but now the focal point has slipped south to an area of shops and supermarkets. The Kidlington we see today is very much a modern creation. The other towns have quite different histories.

The first and most obvious point to note is that the towns are set on main roads and are scattered fairly evenly over the map. In fact, if we broaden the view to take in a greater area of the country, we should find the same pattern repeated over a very large area. It is a pattern which belongs to the rich lowland regions but which is not seen in the poorer uplands. Indeed, the density of towns in an area is one method of gauging that region's historical prosperity. Our area is very much part of the richer zone – not that it is, by any means, to be thought of as just one, consistent, uniform area, for again we find that changes in the structure of the land are reflected in changes in the way in which the land has been used. But, if we had to file all away under one general heading, that heading would read 'agriculture'. Inevitably, such a statement involves the grossest of oversimplification, but it will do to be getting along with until we look more closely at man's work on the land. To understand the town, you have to think your way back into the past.

If you live in a world where the overwhelming requirement is to produce the bare means of living, then those needs will dominate everything that happens in life. At its very simplest, you have a small, entirely self-sufficient community, providing food for survival and materials to cover the body or provide a shelter. You have some employed in producing food and you have craftsmen working on basic raw materials to make them usable by man. Now that is already a pretty complex process, and as societies grow and develop it gets more complex. More specialization sets in. One man may tend the beasts, while another slaughters the animals: some prepare the carcass for food while others treat the hide. You only have to rise a little way above the most primitive society for such complexities to multiply. If the parts are all to fit together, then there must be a meeting-place, somewhere where the tradesman and the farmer can exchange produce and skills. They need a market, and around that market will grow a market town.

Bicester is typical of many such places which simply grew and developed as local needs demanded, without any intervention by planners and designers. It stands at a point where roads meet, an obvious centre if you want to move goods around the country. At this meeting-point you can still see a triangle of roads, with the church set inside the triangle. What you do not get is what you got at Oxford, an obvious pattern of streets. This is what one might call a Topsy town: it just grewed. Two main streets can be seen and, between them, a wavering blue line showing a stream. The triangle of streets also left an obvious gap which could be filled by a market, and though the market-place has been partially filled in, with the first buildings arriving as early as the sixteenth century, the original market is still clearly discernible. This, too, is a pattern

Weavers' cottages at Heptonstall in Yorkshire, easily recognized by the long windows on the upper floor.

that can be found repeated in many areas. With improved communications and an ever greater specialization among markets and traders, the need for huge open markets and fairs diminished. So we find the valuable market-place land at the heart of the town being nibbled away at the edges or filled in at the centre. The permanent shop began to take over from the temporary stall. Bicester's role changed over the years. For a time it was a great centre for sporting gents who came to race horses and hunt. Then the military arrived and imposed their presence on the town, with an airfield to the north and a vast ordnance depot to the south – and the military remain an overwhelming influence in the area. Yet, somehow, through all the changes, the character of the original market town has survived. The market-place still exists: Elizabethan timber-framed houses have not been quite squeezed out by the pressure from their Victorian neighbours.

Witney and Chipping Norton owe their growth and prosperity to quite different factors from those that affected Bicester, even if their origins are similar. Indeed the name 'chipping' means market and the name Witney is equally instructive, for it means 'Witta's Island'. Let us start by looking at the latter. It is sited at a crossing-point on the Windrush and, as the name has already shown and as the contour lines of the map confirm, it is raised up above the low-lying plain with its marshes, bogs and floods. But when we look at the map other names soon suggest new directions of thought. Newland indicates expansion and numerous mills are also shown. Now, the name 'mill' can mean many different things. The commonest use of the word before the eighteenth century was to describe a place where something was ground – corn generally in England and Wales, oats in Scotland,

Cressbrook Mill in Derbyshire, one of the first cotton mills, designed to look like a country mansion.

though the use of the word could be extended to other processes, such as grinding to make gunpowder. There was, however, another type of mill common in the country from medieval times – the fulling mill. Visit Witney today and it will soon become clear just which type of mill was common there. This is a town which belongs less to the main central area of the English Midlands and rather more to the country to the west. It is a town more concerned with sheep and wool than with corn and oats.

One could think of Witney as a medieval new town, much as Oxford was a Saxon new town. It was largely the creation of the Bishop of Winchester, whose patronage helped to raise the town to a prosperous position at some time around the twelfth century. This is the sort of statement that raises more questions than it answers. Even the most powerful prelate could do nothing without the raw materials of success. Witney was well endowed. To the west are the Cotswold Hills, with a soil not particularly well suited to arable farming, but admirable for sheep rearing. The town itself stands clear of the rough hill tracks, set fair and square on the road to London where the wool could be sold. And there is the Windrush flowing through the town. Why did the river make a difference? To understand that, you have to know something of the processing of wool from the sheep's back to make cloth.

To put the process at its simplest, the individual fibres of wool have to be aligned, pulled out and twisted together to make a yarn. The yarn then has to be made into a closely interlocked network by knitting or by weaving. Now, none of this requires any high degree of technology; all the techniques had been known and practised for centuries before Witney was so much as a village. Spinning could be carried out by such basically simple tools as the spindle and whorl, where a falling weight like a spinning top pulls out the fibres and twists them together. This was traditionally women's work – hence spinster. We all have at least a basic idea of what knitting is, and weaving plain cloth is no more complex. But the finished cloth when it came from the loom was greasy, dirty, only loosely woven and liable to shrink. So it needed to be cleaned and pounded or 'felted' to give it body. The earliest means of doing this was to tramp up and down on the cloth in a tub of water – an occupation which gave rise to the surname Walker. The introduction of the water-wheel provided a more efficient way of dealing with the cloth. The wheel turned, tripping large hammers which pounded down on the cloth in a trough below. This was the fulling mill, the final item in the equation that added up to success for Witney.

The town itself is built to a conventional plan, based on a main street, a market square and a large green by the church. All the elements are still there, and so too are the mills, though they are no longer the older-style fulling mills but factories for the manufacture of blankets. Witney moved on with the Industrial Revolution to take work out of cottage and home and into the new spinning and weaving mills. At first, the source of power was, as it had been for the fulling mills, the water-wheel. Look at the map and you can see how the mill buildings are still to be found strung out along the Windrush. Later they would be adapted to steam and

The Early woollen mill in Witney.

then electricity, but the siting still tells of their origin. The Witney weavers survived the onslaught from the north, from Yorkshire and Lancashire, which took away so much of the textile work of the west of England, by specializing in one commodity, blankets. They set up a sound business based to a large extent on export: many a North American Indian chief was persuaded to sign a treaty by the gift of a Witney blanket. There are other names on the map to excite the curious – Newland, for example which is part of Witney yet seems only to have a tenuous connection with the town. It looks like, and was, a village, while the name suggests a piece of deliberate village planning, which appears indeed to have been the case. As happens in so many towns, Witney grew by swallowing smaller neighbours.

Chipping Norton is a market town and like Witney drew much of its prosperity from the wool of Cotswold sheep. It is, in fact, very much a Cotswold town, standing high on a ridge and built of local stone. It too has a market-place, formed from a widened main street. And it too has a woollen mill, in this case a Victorian tweed mill which stopped working in the 1980s. It stands at the edge of the town and is probably the most bizarre building in the entire region. Talk of textile mills and the image that comes to mind is probably, and not unreasonably, that of a square block and towering chimney, surrounded by clusters of terraced houses. This was never the style in the west of England. The mill stands isolated and the building, with its balustraded parapet, might be mistaken for a country mansion if it were not for the factory chimney. This rises from a dome like a giant pepperpot in the centre of the roof. There is nothing like it anywhere else in Britain.

It seems odd to think of this area as being industrialized at all, but this was a busy cloth-producing region from medieval times onwards. However, the Industrial Revolution of the eighteenth century changed the direction of industrial growth quite dramatically. The new centres in Scotland, Wales, northern England and the Black Country produced patterns of a new industrial density. Those who want to see the true effects of the move from cottage work to factory work, from hand power to water power and then steam power, must turn to these other regions. As Witney has shown, however, we have to look for the beginnings in the river valleys where water was available for power. The eighteenth century saw the birth of the first true mill town, based on Richard Arkwright's pioneering cotton mill at Cromford in Derbyshire. But perhaps the most impressive of these early settlements is New Lanark in Scotland, where a mill was built by David Dale, under

Narrow lanes, terraced houses and a mill at the street end: the landscape of the Industrial Revolution at Rawtenstall, Lancashire.

licence from Arkwright, beside the Corra Lin Falls on the Clyde. A new village of tenement blocks was built to house the workforce, and the entire village survives today. This was only a first phase of development. The coming of steam power released the industrialist from the constraints of the river valleys. The factory could be set in the town and the workers could shift for themselves as best they might, and it was in this period that the worst of the grimy industrial slums developed. Speculative builders threw up mean terraces with little concern for sanitation or comfort. The worst have long gone, but the patterns of streets, regulated with blocks of houses pressed close together, can still be seen in the old industrial towns. We shall meet them later on in the walks.

Scattered among the towns we have been looking at are the small towns, villages and hamlets. The smaller settlements can offer just as much variety as the larger – origins to be deduced, patterns of development to be observed and disentangled. From the mass of material set out on our map, let us look at a few examples to get a notion of this rich diversity, starting with the small town of Eynsham, near the Thames. The first thing we notice is that it is not merely close to the river but also close to one of its infrequent crossing-places. It is also separated from the river itself by a complex web of smaller streams: as so often on the upper Thames the nature of the land immediately adjoining the river keeps settlements very much at bay. What can one say about the nature of the town? The map gives very little away. There is a church near the southern edge, and development to the north has clearly been halted by a major road, the A40, and that would seem to be about it. But move to a larger scale or, better still, visit the town itself and some interesting street names soon appear. The most significant of these is Abbey Street, which leads away to the

The local stone slate can still be seen on many houses and cottages in Stonesfield.

south but not, it appears, to anywhere in particular. But the name supplies the answer, for there was an important abbey here, founded in 1005 by the Benedictines. The road itself may fade away but it does continue as a track marking the old and once important road that passed the abbey and linked the town with the river. This gave the town its importance, for the abbey had the right to hold markets and to let out land to tenants for an annual rent. So we find a market and a typical street system which goes with this type of leasehold known as burghage tenure. Where do you look for the oldest street? The High Street is the obvious place and that runs into a second street called Acre End, another very interesting name, suggesting that this was where the town and the old common fields met. The burghage plots can be seen as houses fronting the street with long rectangles of land running away behind them. The end of these plots is marked by a lane that carries a name you will meet in similar village systems throughout the country – Back Lane. The same pattern is seen in Mill Street and, as at Witney, evidence for extension of the town comes in Newland Street, where a second batch of common land was parcelled up and leased out by the abbey. A similar pattern can be found in other towns under the patronage of a great lord or institution, the importance of the town depending on the power of the patron to acquire such rights as the holding of markets.

By no means all towns and villages develop in the same way. Some appear because of particular circumstances. Again names can provide useful hints – though readers should beware of placing too much reliance on place-names, for place-name derivation is an astonishingly complex affair. There are, however, a lot of 'stone' names around, such as Stonesfield, which certainly suggests that quarrying might well have been an activity of some importance. The visitor to Stonesfield will find ample evidence to confirm the notion. The ground slopes away from the village to the south-west and the valley of the Evenlode, and there you can still see piles of spoil, broken stone and disused quarries. Elsewhere you can see, rather more surprisingly, mine entrances, for Stonesfield thrived on underground sources of a special stone which came to carry the name of the village – Stonesfield slate. This is not slate as we normally understand the word, not the thin grey squares from Wales or Cornwall, but a flat limestone which, like slate, can be split for use in roofing. The stone occurs in narrow beds, as much as sixty feet below the surface – hence the mines – but the stone is of such good quality that the effort has always been considered worthwhile. The stone is rougher and cruder than ordinary slate, but contributes a great deal to the special character of the region. Roofs weather and mature, acquiring a rich patina of colour and texture that gives them great visual appeal.

Other village names suggest different origins – Marsh Baldon, for example. It is set on low-lying land cut by the Baldon Brook, so we can reasonably expect it to be, or at any rate to have been, decidedly boggy. On the map you can see a tight group of buildings on high ground, with manor house, church and a few other buildings, including a pub. Beyond that is an open square with houses spread around the edge. A visit reveals the square to be a large village green, the old common land. Even without documentary evidence one can build up what seems to be a sensible sequence of events, starting with a small settlement based on the great house, followed by drainage of the marsh to provide a new common around which houses were then built. Today, it is among the most attractive village greens in the area. A very different sounding name is Charterville, given to an area to the south of Minster Lovell. This is a special case of a planned village of the 1840s, when the Chartists were fighting for reform. It was decided to build a number of villages where industrial workers, tired of a life of factory and town, could start again with a trim new country cottage and a large allotment for growing produce. Where other settlements have developed in apparently random ways, Charterville presents a simple pattern of cottages stretching down the main road.

Sometimes the map provides puzzles. To the north of Oxford, on the banks of the Cherwell, appears the name Hampton Gay. A

The ruined manor house of Hampton Gay.

The distinctive symmetrical styling of a Chartist cottage in Charterville.

church is shown and a single building which, when you visit the spot, turns out to be a rather grand, though ruined, manor house. But the question remains: where is Hampton Gay? The answer can be found by using one's eyes. In the fields by church and manor, under the hooves of grazing cattle, can be seen a series of strange bumps and hollows. It is not easy to detect any pattern on the ground – though it would be simple enough if we could practise levitation and rise a hundred feet above the field. But even with our feet on the ground we can still make out a long straight hollow with ridges enclosing square spaces grouped alongside it. What we are seeing is the last remains of the village. The hollow track was once the main street, the ridges all that remain of house walls, the squares, the platforms on which houses stood. This is only one of literally hundreds of deserted villages throughout Britain. The reasons for their disappearance may often be difficult to disentangle. In a few cases, the scourge of the Black Death left a village so bereft of inhabitants that there were no longer enough left to keep the essential life of the place going. In very many more cases a landowner found more profitable uses for the land than the growing of crops. We shall see more of this both in the Midland counties (see page 105) and at its most ferocious in Scotland (see page 55). Whatever may have happened to cause its abandonment, at Hampton Gay we are seeing a village that died.

Ploughing the land for crops and growing grass for animals to feed on are two of the obvious uses of the land in an agricultural area such as this. They are so much a part of an established system that goes back for hundreds of years that it is easy to believe that the land has always been much as it is now. We shall ignore the aeons of geological time and just look at the comparatively short period during which man has lived in the area. Early man faced a landscape which was vastly different from the world we see around us today. There is a hint of what that world might have been like on the modern map. Spattered over the face of the entire area are a very large number of green splotches indicating woodland, most of which are shown as mixed or deciduous woodland as opposed to the modern softwood plantation. The overall impression is of a wide coverage of woodland which has at some time, possibly remote, possibly recent, been eroded. We simply cannot be precise about any time scale, but research based on the study of pollen remains provides a picture of the past which includes periods of sudden and dramatic change. Forests grew and developed over most of Britain in the years following the end

Coppicing: new shoots are just beginning to appear from the stump or stool.

Here the shoots have grown to a height where the poles can be harvested.

of the Ice Age, when all the familiar woodland trees could be found. Around 3000 BC there was a huge, and still unexplained, decline in the elm population, not dissimilar to that which we are experiencing today. After that, there was a steady and easily explained reduction in woodland coverage. Man began to cut back the trees.

Nevertheless, as we come much closer to our own time, to the medieval period, we find woodland covering a far greater area than we see today. Everyone knows the story of Robin Hood and his men remaining hidden for years in the depths of Sherwood Forest. Today, he would find so little remaining that he could consider himself lucky if he stayed undetected for a day. Sherwood was only one of many great forest areas, one of which was to be found in present day Oxfordshire, the Wychwood Forest. But

The eye catcher at Steeple Aston.

forests and woods were more than simply remnants of uncleared wild country; indeed, it is doubtful if any such wild woodland survived into medieval times. Woods were owned and often carefully managed, an important resource that needed to be tended. Timber was important as a building material, forming the main frame for building. That frame would then be filled in with an interlacing of thin branches – wattle – which would then be daubed with a mixture of straw, clay and manure. The end product was the wattle and daub wall. Wood was needed for fires – coal was mined but until the Industrial Revolution exclusively for industrial purposes. There was a whole range of other uses, such as wood for charcoal and wood for working into hundreds of different objects, from chairs to spoons.

To make maximum use of a woodland area, a balance had to be maintained between trees to be grown to a sufficient size to produce timber for building and wood which could be cut early for other needs. The latter largely depended on coppicing, where the young tree would be allowed to grow and then after a few years would be cut right down almost to ground level. A new growth would then begin from the stump or stool, and the whole process could be repeated. Woods were already being named as an important resource in Domesday Book. Look at an apparently solid block of woodland and you will find that it contains a variety of names. Names in the large one to the south-west of Horton-cum-Studley indicate both ownership – York's Wood, Oakley Wood – and use – Hell Coppice.

Another, equally important, use of woodland in medieval times was as pasture for animals. Some woods were used for pannage, the feeding of swine, which thrived on nuts and acorns; others were preserved as deer parks, in the ownership of either the King or some great lord. The deer parks have certainly left their mark on this particular landscape. Cornbury Park, near Charlbury, occupies a part of the Wychwood Forest and is still shown as a deer park today. The map also has another very evocative name, Grand Vista. A wide, straight path leads into the wood and away from the big house. At once this suggests a more modern and familiar type of park, a place which one looks at and admires, somewhere to stroll and take your leisure. Such areas are shaded grey on the map and there are a surprisingly large number, covering a large area and invariably associated with woodland. These offer a very special type of landscape, but they are by no means insignificant. It is worth looking at two of them, as they rank among the most important examples of this type of landscape in the whole country.

The eighteenth century saw the birth of a new concept, the landscape garden, a garden that was designed to be admired as a microcosm of an idealized world. There were to be miniature seas

The regular arrangement of houses down the main road shows Nuneham Courtenay to be a planned village.

never ruffled by storms, trees artistically placed among meadows, cascades and temples. It was a landscape designed to present nature as a perfect, picturesque composition. Among the first masters of the art was William Kent, who, early in the eighteenth century, designed the garden at Rousham. The first feature of note, and one which was to give a whole series of gardens their special character, is the ha-ha, the sunken boundary fence. It creates the illusion of the garden extending without a break into the surrounding countryside. The garden itself has a fine lawn and then a series of terraces descending towards the Cherwell. Down by the lake is a classical temple, built in imitation of the then fashionable ruins of Rome, which the English gentry had discovered in their grand tours of Europe. It is a landscape planned in terms of views, and unless you think of the garden as the centrepiece of the whole landscape another prominent feature will never make sense. In the middle of a field at Steeple Aston is a huge wall, with arches and buttresses. Yet there seem to be no other remains, not even a sign of other walls. It is, in fact, an eye-catcher, a mock ruin set at just that point to produce the best possible effect when viewed from the lawns of Rousham. It had been decided that the vista from the house needed a ruin and, as no one had been sufficiently accommodating as to provide a real one, this mock ruin was constructed.

Landscaping on a far grander scale can be seen at Blenheim. Here a large part of the countryside was radically altered to suit the designer's taste. The present estate was born out of the former deer park belonging to the manor house of Woodstock. Then Sir John Vanbrugh designed the present Blenheim Palace for the Marlboroughs and Lancelot 'Capability' Brown produced the park. The old Woodstock Manor was pulled down, in spite of Vanbrugh's pleas to the Duchess of Marlborough for its retention – 'this paper has something ridiculous in it' was her comment on the proposal. The River Glyme was dammed to create a lake, crossed by an elegant bridge, and over 2,000 acres were enclosed within the park walls. This major restructuring of the landscape to force it to conform to a pictorial ideal is only part of the story, for the park, in its earlier existence as a deer park, had had other effects.

The village of Woodstock had in ancient times been situated within what was to be the park area, and it was peremptorily removed on the orders of the lord of the manor. This resettled village is old Woodstock. Then, in the twelfth century, Henry II, a frequent visitor to Woodstock Manor, handed out part of the wasteland on the edge of the estate for the foundation of a new market town – New Woodstock. The two settlements still retain their distinct identities. In the eighteenth century villages such as Kirtlington were similarly changed to make room for a park. A particularly interesting example is Nuneham Courtenay, where the entire village was demolished and a new model village built on the main road. Its origins as a planned village are immediately apparent in the uniformity of the overall plan and the uniformity of building style. The movement towards emparkment produced many planned villages – though few landlords showed the ruthlessness of the Harcourts of Nuneham Courtenay.

When the ancient woodland was cleared, there began a steady process of turning the wasteland to agricultural land; but the landscape we see today is mostly of far more recent origin. It is the landscape of enclosure, when the open fields were closed off by hedgerows so that better farming techniques could be employed, or to enable arable land to be converted to pasture. The former ensured better land use for crops; the latter spelt death to many villages. The earliest enclosures were by consent, though given the power of the landlord and the comparatively weak position of the villagers consent must often have been a somewhat euphemistic description of the process. Such enclosures were begun in Tudor times, and continued in the eighteenth and nineteenth centuries by parliamentary enclosures, when Enclosure Acts were obtained and the land parcelled out into neat pieces by official decree. All of this great change gave us the 'traditional' countryside of field and hedgerow with which we are all familiar. If, however, we want to catch a glimpse of an earlier age, we have to turn our attention to those areas where enclosure turned land from arable into pasture. The grass grew over the old plough land, setting its patterns in ridges and hollows that can still be seen today.

The commonest pattern of these 'fossilized' landscapes are the signs of ridge and furrow, showing a medieval field pattern which we shall look at in detail on our walks (see page 103). Not all land lends itself to this sort of treatment. Steep hillsides present special problems and here the medieval farmer produced strip lynchets, which appear now as terraces following the contours of the hill. You can see them on the edge of the Cotswolds, along the River Glyme between Lidstone and Old Chalford, where there is also a fine series of dips and bumps marking the site of a deserted village.

But those who wish to look back even further in time will have to leave this area altogether to hunt for what are misleadingly known as Celtic field systems. These are quite small fields which rarely have anything to do with the Celts, and which date back into prehistory. They are small because of the limited power available for ploughing, which was often provided by the farmer himself, and their edges are marked by ridges. They can be found in many parts of the country, often accompanied by fields for grazing. A particularly fine example is based on the Bronze Age village of Standon Down in Cornwall.

The cultivation of crops remains the basis of human life for much of our planet, but crops need to be treated as well as grown. Barns are required for storage, and for the main crops of Britain some form of grinding device is needed to turn the grain into usable flour or meal. The grain mill was an essential element in the country's economy. Domesday Book records more than 5,000 mills, a few of which might have been worked by animals, but the great majority would have been powered by the water-wheel. This device came to Britain in two quite different forms. There was the

The click or Norse mill: the paddles turn directly in the stream and the grindstones above them move at the same speed.

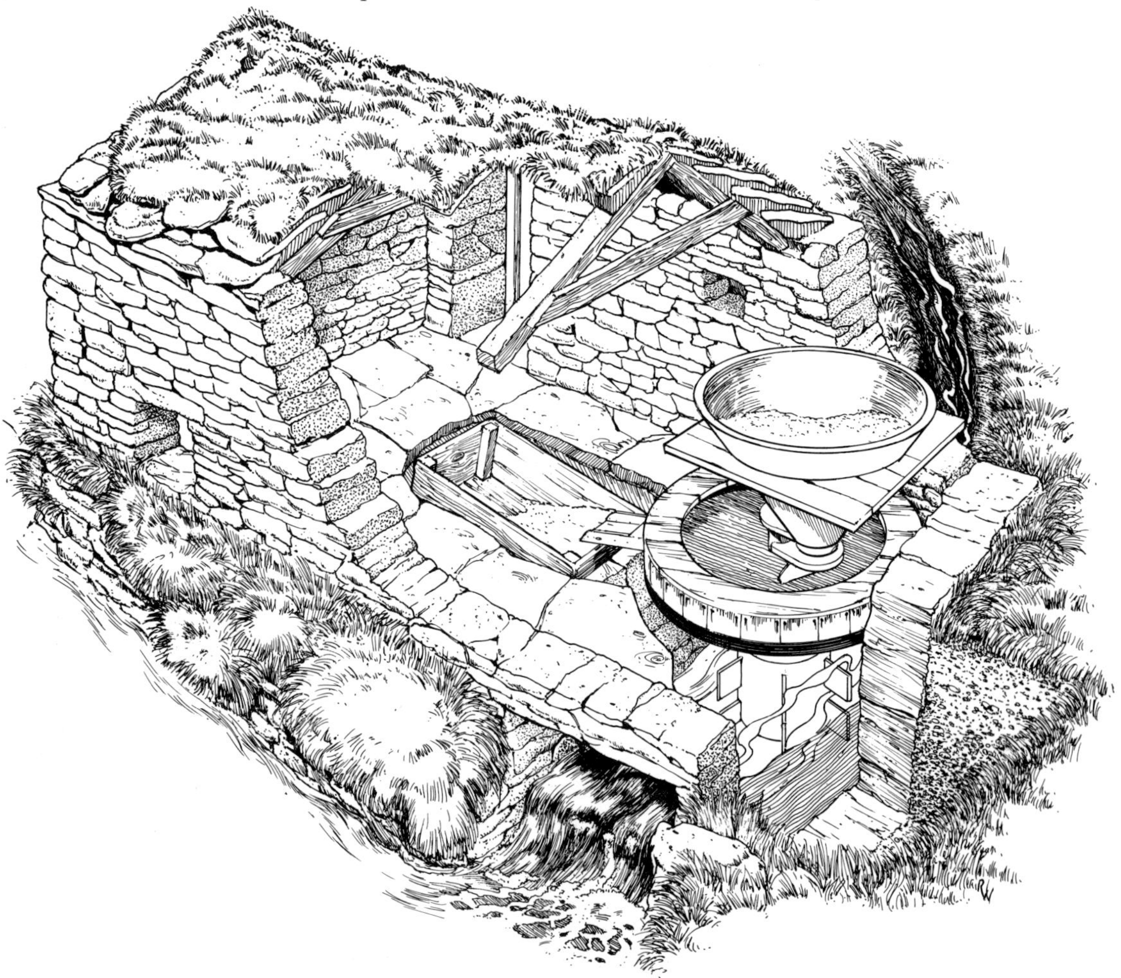

The water-powered grain mill, Venn Mill, shows traditional weatherboarding.

vertical wheel in which the paddles were set on the rim of a wheel turning around a horizontal axis, and this type was almost certainly first brought to Britain by the Romans. It was to prove capable of development into a very efficient and sophisticated device. There are many surviving examples of this type of mill throughout the country. The other form is far simpler – the Norse mill, brought to these shores by the Vikings. Here a vertical shaft with paddles dips down into a stream and supplies a direct drive to the machinery. Norse mills are rare but one can still find them in the more distant corners of the land, a particularly fine example being the Dounby Mill in Orkney. This is a minute building with the simplest of machinery, just a pair of grindstones set on the spinning shaft. Our Oxford map shows plenty of water mills, such as Venn Mill, north

Old gear wheels stand outside Venn water mill waiting for the restorers.

of East Hanney. All are of the more usual type. The water mill is in fact a very important building in the story of developing technology, for it brought a power greater than that of the strongest animals, and it brought control of that power through the use of gearing. The water mill did, however, require an ensured regular supply of water, and it was necessary to block rivers and streams with weirs. The water had to be tamed before it was brought to the wheel by the use of artificial channels, or leats, controlled by sluices. Once the water reached the mill, however, and the wheel was turning, it could power other things beside grindstones. At Combe you will find the maintenance works for the Blenheim Estate. Here the wheel powered a sawmill, a woodworking shop and a forge. Later, in a fine belt-and-braces exercise, a steam engine was installed to take over in times of drought.

In some areas, the water-wheel gave way to the windmill. There is a fine example at Brill – just the sort of airy hilltop position that suited the windmill. While the watermill can be traced back to Roman and Viking, there are no records of windmills existing in Britain before the twelfth century. The earliest form of such mills is the post-mill, so called because the main building pivots on a central post. Windmill sails will only go round if they are turned to the wind, so in the post-mill the buck, the main structure with all the machinery inside and sails outside, is moved round as required. That is what we find at Brill. Later mills made the job of positioning the sails somewhat easier by attaching them to a rotating cap – set on a brick or stone base in tower mills, or on a wooden housing in smock mills. Where they survive intact windmills make fascinating features in the landscape, but the derelict bases of tower mills are more frequently met.

The uses of the land vary quite considerably from place to place, even when we are looking at such a comparatively small area as this. In the western part we find much of the land given over to pasture, while other regions are largely arable or mixed farming. It all depends on the nature of the land and the soil. The stony ground of the Cotswolds is clearly less suited to crops than the rich soils further to the east. Then there is the special case of the wetland. The most interesting example is Otmoor, an area totally devoid of any form of building, but criss-crossed by water channels. On the map the River Ray appears on one edge as a straight blue line, labelled New River Ray. This is clearly an area where man has interfered a great deal with the landscape. In fact, the Otmoor we see today is the product of a long period of change in which the Ray was rerouted, large-scale drainage was undertaken and the old common land of the moor was enclosed. It was not a peaceful process. The local villagers objected violently to the loss of their rights to graze geese and cattle, and riots flared up throughout the 1830s. The villagers' view was expressed in a verse of the time:

Saxstead Green mill in Suffolk, a sophisticated post-mill: the whole of the main structure pivots on a central post and the sails are automatically turned into the wind by the vane set above the foot of the steps.

The fault is great in man or woman,
That steals a goose from off the common.
But what can plead that man's excuse,
That steals the common from the goose?

Enclosures, which changed so much of the country, and produced undoubted benefits by increasing the productivity of the land, also brought frequent hardship by taking away the meagre rights of the poorest of the people.

Agriculture still predominates in this area, but there were many other land uses. Stone has already been mentioned, and the numerous quarries, but the area can boast one special stone with a particular use. In the more northern area you can see buildings constructed of a lovely, rich, golden-brown stone, which derives its colour from the presence of iron. Ironstone gave rise to one of the area's few industries, though you will find little evidence for it on the map or even on the ground. However, just off the northern edge of the map is Hook Norton, where the Brymbo Ironworks were established. The region was never exploited in the way that South Wales, say, which could boast both iron ore and coal for the smelters, was exploited. And, though there are many signs of ironstone workings, they are not obviously different from other quarries of the region. One other commodity which the area does possess in abundance is gravel and the flooded gravel pits are now among the most prominent features of the landscape. Unlike the ironstone workings, these are still very much a going concern and are likely to be worked into the foreseeable future. And when work finishes we are left with the problem of what to do with these artificial lakes and their barren surroundings.

Land use will inevitably present quite different aspects in different regions. There are obviously vast differences between, say, the Scottish Highlands and the agricultural land of the Midlands; there are no less pronounced variations as you move from rural to industrial areas. Coastal regions may turn away from the land altogether and look to the sea for their livelihood, to fishing or trade. All regions do have one thing in common: patterns of development will have been affected by their place in the communication system of the country. And changes in communication patterns, covering the full period from prehistory to the present age, are there to be read on the map.

As always when looking at the landscape, it is the earliest evidence that is most difficult to find and interpret. There is ample evidence that prehistoric man moved around the country a great deal. Suitable stone for shaping into implements in the neolithic period was not universally available: an axe fashioned from the crumbling limestone of the Cotswolds would be quite useless. Yet stone axes were used and must have been brought to the area from other parts of the country. The best known site for flints is Grimes Graves in Norfolk, where a complex system of mines has been discovered. Flints from this area have been identified over a wide area of Britain. The assumption is that there must have been well established trade routes, and tradition supports the view. Where would you expect to find such routes? The answer must be, on the ridges of high ground that would keep the travellers clear of the wet, muddy river valleys. To the south of our area, we have the

A neat, workmanlike stone culvert carries drainage water beneath the Roman road of Wade's Causeway, Goathland.

Ridgeway, running across the Berkshire Downs. It has long been asserted that the use of this ridge as a track goes back far beyond written records. But when we look at it there is nothing in the physical landscape that says anything other than that man walks this track now and has done so in the past. No doubt those who came this way with their goods or their animals left their mark, but as others trod the same path for generation after generation the old marks successively disappeared as new were added. It is very rare indeed to find any trace at all of what we might call hard physical evidence for ancient trackways – rare, but not impossible. In the boggy ground to the north of the Polden Hills in Somerset, excavations revealed a system of causeways built across the marsh to join settlements on the islands of higher ground. Some causeways consisted of brushwood hurdles held down by pegs, while others were made of split logs. The enveloping peat preserved them and modern radio-carbon techniques have dated them to around 3000 BC. A section of brushwood hurdling can be seen in the Woodspring Museum at Weston-super-Mare.

Evidence about roads becomes a little easier to obtain as we get nearer the present time, when roads became something more than the tracks that most people followed. Once men began surfacing roads and building bridges – in other words, producing structures that survived – then the story becomes much clearer. The most famous of the early road builders were the Romans. Textbooks used to tell us that all roads led to Rome and that they were all straight: neither statement is, alas, altogether true. Roman roads cut across the country in all directions, and although the majority appear as more or less straight lines the Romans, like later generations of engineers, were forced to provide a zigzagging route when faced with exceptionally hilly country. There is a corollary to this, which is of some importance to landscape detectives. Just as not all Roman roads are straight, so not all straight roads are Roman. A quick look at the map would suggest that the road running from south-west to north-east through Bicester is Roman. Well, the northerly part of the A421 does indeed follow a Roman alignment, but the equally straight section to the south does not. In fact, the most important of the Roman roads in the area, Akeman Street, which ran from St Albans to Cirencester, is far more difficult to spot. It is fairly plain as the A41 from the east, but elsewhere it appears only as minor roads and footpaths. In any case, it gives us little idea of what a Roman road was like, how it was surveyed, built and surfaced. To see such a road in anything like its original condition we have to travel to Goathland in the North

Yorkshire Moors, to the road known as Wade's Causeway – a very misleading name, for it suggests a connection with General Wade, who supervised road construction in the Scottish Highlands in the eighteenth century. The road, however, is very definitely Roman, and shows many of the main characteristics of Roman construction. For a start, it is raised on a little embankment, known as an aggar, which lifts it above the surroundings and aids drainage. A great deal of care was taken to ensure that the water that flowed freely over this high moorland did not damage the aggar. Culverts were constructed to pierce the bank, each one being lined with stone. The surface of the road remains remarkably well preserved in many places, and can be seen to consist of very large stone slabs, which were probably covered by gravel. Wade's Causeway is a very minor road compared with the main thoroughfares, but the care taken over its construction shows just what a fine system the Romans created in their brief occupation of Britain. Nothing of comparable quality was to be built for well over a thousand years.

Once we leave the Roman period, it is extremely difficult to define a road as having its origins in any one period, for once a route became well established it was used and modified by succeeding generations. So there is nothing on the modern map – and often little on the ground – to show that a modern road had its origins in Saxon times, Tudor times or even later. There are, however, places where roads unexpectedly turn off a modern route and then appear to vanish from sight, which suggests that we might be looking at an old road that has been abandoned after some change in alignment. Such a road can be seen in the north-west corner of the map, running off the B4026 at Chalford Green. It appears first as a minor road or track and then continues as a footpath which crosses the Glyme and heads off to Chipping Norton. It begins as something more than a mere footpath, and a visit reveals a wide trackway running between walls and hedges.

The presence of a boundary hedge along a road can be a great help in determining its age. Dr Max Hooper produced a hedge-dating technique in 1970. Take a length of hedge and then count the number of species of trees and shrubs in a 30-metre section. Repeat this for a number of sections, take an average of the results, multiply by 100 and you have the age of the hedge. Six species would indicate that a hedge was 600 years old, seven species, 700 years, and so on. There is no basis for the theory other than observation and it is not infallible – a local history group recently did a hedge dating and came up with a figure of six species but later research showed the hedge to have been planted in the eighteenth century. That was an exception: in general, fieldwork accords well with documentary evidence. So, to return to our road to Chipping Norton, there is every indication that this is a medieval hedge beside a medieval road. It was in fact the highway between Enstone and Chipping Norton.

Other ancient highways have remained in use. The A34 which runs south from Oxford is based on a major Saxon route from Winchester, though the section we can see on the map has none of the marks of a major medieval route, for it studiously avoids every town along the way. In fact it is very clear from its banks and complex interchanges that this is a road of the twentieth century, designed to hurry traffic along by dual carriageway and bypass. The old A34 ran from the centre of Oxford down what is now a minor road to Abingdon and then on the present B4017 through Drayton and Steventon. This is by no means the only road in the area that has been overtaken by the changing needs of the age of the internal combustion engine. The B4027 turns off the A40 to pass to the east of Oxford. Travellers along the way will soon see that although it is now a minor road it has remarkably wide grass verges, suggesting that it was once considerably broader than it is at present. A further hint of antiquity was, until recently, to be seen near Beckley, where a stone marker showed the boundary between parishes responsible for the upkeep of the road. Until at least the eighteenth century this was the usual method of ensuring that roads were kept in good condition. That at least was the theory. Male parishioners were required to put in six days work a year: contemporary complaints suggest that these unwilling labourers usually put in six days drinking instead. It is rather sad that the stone has now gone, along with many other relics that might remind us that this was once the main road from London to Worcester.

Other signs of antiquity can be found at river crossings. An old bridge must imply an old road. The oldest bridge in the district lies just off our map – Radcot Bridge, which crosses the upper Thames and was first recorded in 1209. The old bridge is a steeply rising structure that crosses a backwater; the main channel is crossed by an eighteenth-century bridge. The line of a road can also give a hint as to age. The minor roads around Sunningwell bend and twist, often turning through right angles. This is because they follow old field boundaries, the furlongs of the medieval system. The name Green Lane appears, a name which often relates to ancient estate boundaries. In other regions there are more obvious indications of antiquity. The sunken lanes of the West

Country with their high hedge banks are often very old, so old that there is seldom any way in which they can be dated. Boundary banks defined the routes for the lanes and generations of users plodded away, sinking the lanes ever lower into the land.

The packhorse route and the drove road were other important communication links. Long trains of pack animals were used in, for example, the woollen trade, carrying fleeces one way and cloth the other. The commonest sign of their presence is the packhorse bridge, narrow, steeply rising and with a low parapet to allow the packs slung on either side of the animals to pass across. These routes can be traced quite easily, for they often crossed open

Simple, functional design characterized early canal structures such as Pigeon Lock on the Oxford Canal.

moorland and you can still find cobbled pathways to help the passage over steep hillsides. Drove roads are less easy to discern, though there are still signs to be seen – lonely pubs with names such as Drovers' Arms, road names such as Welsh Way near Banbury, indicating the route taken by the Welsh drovers bringing their beasts to English markets.

The modern system of surfaced roads dates back to the eighteenth century, beginning with the famous military roads of Scotland, built under the direction of General Wade to aid troop movements at the time of the Jacobite rebellion. The finest survivor from that time is the bridge at Aberfeldy (see page 59). But it was the turnpike road that brought a major difference to travel in Britain. These were roads that, in theory at least, were given a decent surface and travellers were made to pay tolls to cover the cost of construction. Under the turnpike system such great engineering works as Telford's suspension bridge across the Menai Straits were constructed. The new age brought in the mail coach and the stage coach, and with them the coaching inn. It also brought many changes on a smaller scale, which can be spotted in the modern landscape. Turnpikes were authorized by Act of Parliament, and the law laid down what tolls could be collected and stipulated that the roads should be furnished with such useful features as milestones and signposts. Tolls were collected at toll-houses, usually set at crossroads or near the end of the new roads. A surviving example can be seen at the Oxford ends of the Banbury Road. It is, like its fellows, easily recognized, for it is a hexagonal building, jutting out into the road, with windows facing up and down the way where traffic would come. A blank space on the first floor of the side facing the road would originally have held a board listing the tolls. The system has not quite disappeared, for tolls are still collected from drivers using the bridge over the Thames at Swinford. Milestones too can still be spotted, often rather grand, handsome affairs.

Change continues still on the road as the system is continuously adapted to meet the needs of modern traffic. The bypass, the dual carriageway and the motorway are today's contribution to the landscape. And, just as the turnpikes aroused controversy in their day, so now the motorway has its opponents and supporters. At the time of writing, arguments are still going on over a new motorway planned for the Cherwell Valley. If the scheme goes ahead, its visual impact on the region will be immense, and among the sufferers will be another transport system which developed in the eighteenth century, the Oxford Canal.

A typical toll-house facing out into the main road. This example is from the Holyhead Road.

In the days when all transport depended on natural power for movement – animals for haulage, wind for sails – water transport represented far and away the most efficient system in the country. In terms of fuel costs, it still does, but that is another story. In a period that stretches back into prehistory, the boat held an advantage over all other vehicles. Ships were the only method of getting from Britain to the rest of the world, and major cities such as London grew up around the ports and the port facilities. Inland, the navigable river was the most important trading route and the Thames was among the principal highways of the country. Like the ports established for seagoing vessels, so too the inland port formed an important nucleus for development. Not everywhere, however, was blessed with a river and the riverless areas included such important regions as the Midlands around Birmingham. If water transport was demonstrably cheaper than road transport and no natural waterway existed, then the answer had to lie with artificial waterways. In the eighteenth century the age of the canal was born.

The use of the lock to raise and lower craft on waterways was established on river navigations long before the eighteenth century. The eighteenth-century contribution lay in using the lock and an artificial channel to join the parts of the river system together. One of the principal engineers of the early days of canal construction was James Brindley, and the Oxford Canal begun under his direction in 1769 is a splendid example of his ideas put into practice. It can be seen on our map wriggling its way up beside the Cherwell, receiving regular steps up through its many well spaced locks. It continues to follow the Cherwell in this way up beyond Banbury, where Brindley then had to cross a watershed to head down to the river systems of the north. Faced by hills and hollows, valleys and ridges, he set out to try to keep his canal on the level by following the natural contours. This involved an incredibly tortuous course culminating at the hill of Wormleighton, which the canal almost encompasses, more like a moat than a transport route. At last the struggle to maintain a level was abandoned, and the canal charges downhill through a flight of locks at Napton. One other feature deserves special mention – the small lake beside the canal where it is crossed by the A43 at Oxford. This is not, in fact, a natural lake at all but a reservoir, an essential part of the canal system. Every time a lock is emptied the water passes into the next stretch of canal, then into the next lock and so on down until it is lost in the river. All that water has to be replaced, hence the need for reservoirs.

Later canals used far bolder techniques – deep cuttings sliced through hills, high embankments carried canals over valleys, aqueducts crossed rivers and tunnels pierced hills. The canals were instrumental in speeding the heavy goods needed by the burgeoning Industrial Revolution, but do not themselves have any very dramatic impact on the landscape. When a canal closes, as did the Wilts and Berks that joined the Thames at Abingdon, it can require real detective work to locate even a trace of it. And although the Oxford Canal is still busy with pleasure boats it creates little visual impact. Its effects on the surroundings, however, are there to be seen. At Thrupp, for example, a small settlement of canal cottages was established and other new settlements grew up at other important points. A significant name appears on the map close to the canal – Gibraltar. Gibraltar suggests rock, rock suggests quarrying and quarrying suggests just the kind of bulk goods to which the canal was ideally suited. So we find the quarry, an extensive wharf, houses and a canalside pub. In fact the effects of the canal are more widespread than at first appears. Offering as it did the first opportunity for moving heavy cargo at low cost, it began the trend towards standardization that continues to this day. Building materials no longer had to be those that were locally available. Midland thatch could be replaced by Welsh slate, local stone by mass-produced brick. It was a process of erosion of local identity that was to accelerate as the canal age gave way to the railway age.

The great impact made by the railways is reflected by railway lines on the map – a series of black lines criss-crossing, running from side to side and top to bottom. And these are just the working lines, in among which are the paler shadows of former glories, the disused railways. In its heyday, this was a region dominated by the Great Western Railway. Brunel's original main line from London to Bristol can be seen slicing across the bottom of the map with major extensions running through Oxford to Birmingham and to Worcester through Charlbury. Add to those the numerous branch lines, often victims of the famous Beeching axe, and you have an inkling of the size of the Great Western empire. It does not, however, monopolize the map. The London North Western line cuts down through Bicester, and there were once other railways in the region which do not figure at all on modern maps, such as the route to Brill, which came in from the east. The civil engineering involved in such a network must necessarily become a major feature in the land, but the effect is more pronounced than that. Just as the canals gave birth to canal settlements, so the railways had their own towns. Didcot was dramatically changed and expanded with a rush of new housebuilding when it became a major railway junction. And the genuine railway new towns, such as Swindon to the south, were built to an even more impressive scale.

The railways continued the process of change begun on the canals. The movement of materials became progressively quicker

Didcot, with the lines of the old Great Western Railway and the great cooling towers of the power station.

and cheaper. Industry grew, towns developed and, just as important, there was an acceleration in the movement of ideas. The sleepy market town suddenly became part of a busier, bustling world. The town with a railway attracted investment and began to grow: the town without began to dwindle and decline. Whole areas of the country were open to new influences. The railway brought holidaymakers out of the industrial areas and encouraged the growth of the seaside resort. Even the remotest wilderness now seemed to be within reach of the railway, as anyone who has ever stood on Rannoch station surrounded by tracts of apparently empty moorland can testify. The whole pattern of life has changed, even if that change cannot always be read as physical marks on the ground.

A line of stone sleeper blocks showing the holes where the rails of a tramway were spiked into place. These are on an early railway at Portland, Dorset.

How did the railway age begin? In attempting to answer that question we have to go back to the industrial landscape of the eighteenth century. The canals were fine as far as they went, but in really hilly or mountainous country canal building is an impossibility. So simple railways were constructed. Trucks were pulled by horses and the hills were overcome by the use of stationary steam engines, sited on the top, which hauled the trucks up by cable – gravity took care of the downhill journey. These early railways are known as tramways or plateways and the cable-worked sections are inclined planes. We shall be meeting their physical remains on our walks. It was on such a tramway, the Penydarren in South Wales, that the first steam locomotive ran over rails in 1804; the prelude to the railway age had been played. The main drama had to wait a little while, as the steam locomotive began its career hauling coal at north-eastern collieries before the first passenger line was established in the 1820s. The Great Western Railway was authorized by Act of Parliament in 1835.

The decline of the railways has coincided with the rise of motor transport on the roads, and that might seem to be the end of what we shall be looking for in terms of transport and the landscape. The twentieth century, however, still has one more story to add, the story of air travel. We do not usually think of this as having a very marked effect, yet our map shows no fewer than ten airfields, some disused, some still very much in use. They are all, with the exception of Oxford Airport, military installations, and they occupy a very substantial acreage. Their effects extend beyond the obvious ones of being home to large, noisy machines. They also require complex radio and electronic installations to keep them functioning and these can dominate large tracts of countryside. Unlike the other transport systems, the nature of air travel – the need for large, flat areas for airports – means that not all areas of the country are affected to the same degree. But even this most modern transport development is not always obtrusive. Old wartime bases fall into disuse and that detective instinct will be needed again if they are to be recognized for what they are.

One of the great appeals of landscape detecting lies in this tremendous variety. One moment you are pondering over a building that turns out to be part of a Second World War airbase, the next you are looking at the remnants of the Stone Age. A hump in the ground might turn out to be an air-raid shelter or a Bronze Age burial chamber.

This one map has provided a fund of information from which we have been able to build up a general picture of the land and its

A house that still shows its origins, particularly in the canopy at the front. This was formerly Upton station on the Didcot, Newbury and Southampton Junction Railway.

history. But it has been a picture painted with only the broadest of strokes, scarcely more than a blocking in of the principal shapes. The area is quite simply too large for any details to show. The map is a starting-point for investigation, but no more than that. You can look at it and say to yourself 'That is an area that looks as if it could have something interesting to show', but you have to go there yourself and walk the ground to see the real clues to the past. It would be possible to give a series of general guidelines to how such an investigation might be carried out, but we have preferred to try and show by example. That is, after all, how most of us – and certainly it is true of both authors – start to gain an interest. We see things and then we start asking questions. What is it? Why is it there? What does it signify? So now we should like to invite you to join us on the trail, on twelve walks in different parts of Britain, to see what we saw and then to follow up the clues to some sort of understanding of the changes that have gone towards making the landscape we see today.

ON THE TRAIL

The twelve walks that make up this section have been chosen to give as wide a range of scenery and historical evidence as possible. Happily, they are not unique – we could have chosen another dozen, or another, or another. And, although each walk is

primarily concerned with a particular theme, the walks never, in practice, fitted quite so neatly into the prearranged pattern. So we set off on a walk to investigate Iron Age settlements and found ourselves puzzling over a nineteenth-century industrial site, a walk to ancient fortifications disclosed an intriguing railway, and so it went on for walk after walk. And that, in the end, was one of the great attractions of the walks – their ability to surprise, to turn up the unsuspected evidence of a previously unconsidered past. We found ourselves playing the roles of landscape detectives in earnest, puzzling over the evidence, trying to draw conclusions and then going on to check and confirm our theories. No doubt those who choose to follow our particular tracks will find their own evidence and draw their own conclusions, just as those who devise walks of their own will find surprises and puzzles as we have done. We hope that the walks will give the reader as much pleasure as they have given the authors – but they will only do so if the walker goes properly prepared.

The first essential is to be adequately clad, and this is particularly essential for those walks which take in hill country. Map and compass – and the ability to use both – are essential. The appropriate 1:50000 Ordnance Survey maps are listed for each walk. Good walking boots and weatherproof clothing are equally important. Anyone who doubts this should have accompanied us on our first walk, when spring sunshine disappeared, the wind howled and snow clouds gathered. A notice at the visitor centre at the foot of Ben Lawers pointed out another requirement – good legs, to which they might have added strong lungs. None of the walks is unduly arduous, but none should be taken lightly – though the town walks obviously come into a different category from the others. One thing we can say with assurance: if you cope well with the first on the list, you will have nothing to worry about with the rest.

WALK 1

A NATURAL LANDSCAPE

Route: *Ben Lawers Visitor Centre to Beinn Ghlas summit and back (8 miles)*

Map: *OS Sheet 51 (1:50 000 series)*

Stand by Loch Tay and look up at the peak of Ben Lawers and what you see appears to be a completely wild landscape, totally unchanged by man. True, those with good vision and a discerning eye will spot a footpath snaking through the heather, but it is easy to believe that little else has changed not just over the years but over the centuries as well. That first impression is a delusion. Far from being a totally natural landscape, this is countryside that has been changed and adapted quite drastically in order to fit it to human needs. Those changes can be deduced from a careful observation of the modern landscape.

Our route starts on the north shore of Loch Tay, where a narrow road leads up the hill to the National Trust for Scotland's visitor centre. The first part of our walk follows a nature trail laid out by the trust, with points of interest carefully signposted along the way. This is a great help for those who might, at first, feel a little uncertain about their ability to recognize features from simple descriptions. The nature trail is a little over a mile and a half in length, and offers a gentle stroll with time to look and inspect without the exertion needed for the longer route. A good deal can be seen without climbing to the top of the mountain, but the gains from making the effort are nevertheless very real.

The route from the visitor centre is along a series of duckboards laid over the peat bog. The peat is formed as part of a long process which has its origins in the hardness of the local rocks. Slow to weather, with few minerals dissolving out of them, they form thin, acid soils. A few plants will grow, but because of the acidity the bacteria and fungi which cause decay are absent. So the plants decompose only partially and this partial decomposition leads to the formation of peat. This is definitely not good agricultural land

The 'wild' landscape of Ben Lawers.

for crops, and if you look at the bog plants you will see how some have become specially adapted to ensure they get the nutrients they need for survival. The most spectacular is the sundew, a plant with leaves covered in tentacles which can trap insects that land on them. When an insect is held, the other tentacles curl round it, the leaf folds up and the insect is, literally, digested by the plant. No surprise then to find that man has been unable to grow crops here. But the peat has its uses as will become clear later on in the walk.

The path leads on to a burn, where the track divides, one route following each bank of the small mountain stream. Here we have our first indication that our natural world is not what it seems. First, the stream itself in its deep ravine, the Edramucky Burn, seems to have a wider and deeper channel than the somewhat pathetic trickle of water would lead you to expect. So you might well think that it has been interfered with in some way – a theory that will soon be confirmed. There are more lessons yet to be learned at this spot. The steep ravine sides show a richness and variety of plant life that is absent from the surrounding hills. In particular, you will find a great many species such as wood anemone and wood sorrel, commonly associated with woodland. The explanation is not very hard to find, for in summer you will see sheep all over the upland region. There may not seem to be many, for they spread far across the mountain, but in fact something like eight thousand sheep graze on Ben Lawers. And eight thousand sheep grazing even over such a very large area have a pronounced effect on plant growth. Clear away the sheep, and the whole mountain would change dramatically in appearance. The ravine provides the clue to what would happen for here the sheep cannot reach. Quite soon scrub would begin to appear in the area, and the woodland plants would gain a hold. Before man came and began the work of clearance, this was a forest.

Already, then, we have considerable evidence of man's effect on

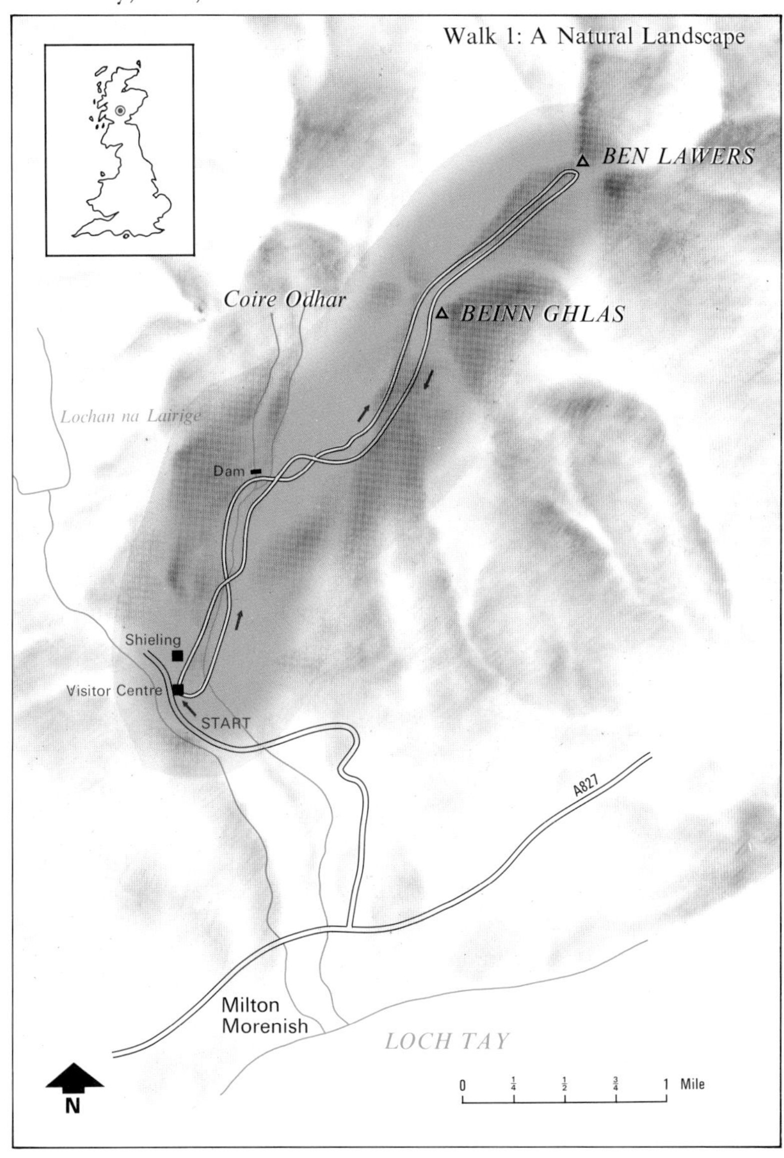

this apparently untouched landscape, and there is still more information to be gleaned from this small area. Close by the track you can see the low walls of rectangular stone buildings. They are not big enough for animals, nor would they seem adequate for even the poorest of families, but would be sufficient for the needs of individuals. There are no signs of fields or gardens, but the buildings are set close to running water and one could well assume that they were home to herdsmen or shepherds. They are, in fact, shielings. Once the whole Tay valley consisted of hundreds of small farms where crops were grown and cattle kept. In order to keep the cattle from the crops and to take advantage of the upland

The tumbled boulders of the dry stream bed.

Living clues to the nature of the present landscape: the sheep that graze its slopes.

grazing, the cattle were taken up the mountain in the spring and there they stayed until the crops were harvested and the weather began to deteriorate towards winter. On the mountain they had to be tended and the cows needed to be milked, so these simple huts were built as summer homes for the graziers. The walls were low, and the roof consisted of a framework of branches covered by turf. Now the thick stone walls survive, as do the tracks, zigzagging up the hill, worn by generations of these summer herders. The path up the western bank of the stream is a typical shieling track. This system of grazing is known as transhumance, and the state of collapse of the shielings suggests that it has long been ended. Certainly there are now no cattle to be seen grazing the hillside, just sheep. It was the sheep, in fact, that brought the system to an end. The landowners of the nineteenth century decided that there was a profit to be made from the introduction of sheep to the Highlands. The small farmers were dispossessed, the cattle removed and the sheep moved in. This was the time of the infamous Highland Clearances, which drove thousands from their homes. The ruined shielings remain as evidence of a way of life that ended nearly two centuries ago.

The path continues up the eastern side of the stream, and it is worth noting the care that has been taken to retain the nature of the countryside intact. Drainage is mainly by concealed wooden ducting, and the stream is bridged in the simplest way by laying flat slabs of stone across it. Man may have altered the landscape by creating a pathway, but he has done so very unobtrusively. When you reach the point where the very obvious trail leads off to Ben Lawers, more obtrusive signs appear. First, the reason for the lack

The ruins of a shieling where a herdsman lived while tending animals grazing on the hills in summer.

of water is now apparent, for the stream is dammed, the flow controlled through sluices. The water disappears underground and is, in fact, carried to Lochan na Lairige, where it joins water from similarly dammed mountain streams to build up a reservoir to feed the Killin hydroelectric power station. Other signs of interference with the natural order can be discerned from here but as many of them are more easily seen from a higher vantage point we will look at them later. To reach that higher point now involves a long slog and a steep climb. The path to Ben Lawers is at least obvious – too obvious in fact, for the modern enthusiasm for hill walking has resulted in serious erosion. Walkers are being encouraged to take diversions in order to give the plants a chance to re-establish themselves. There has been some success. Look, for example, for purple saxifrage among the rocks, a tiny but robust plant with attractive mauve flowers. Look out, too, for the ski hut on the southern slope of Coire Odhar, another sign of the new leisure use – or not so new in this case, for it was built in 1932, the first in Scotland.

If you find you are not quite so fit as you thought you were, you will be glad of the opportunity to pause in the walk to take in more details of the landscape. By the time you reach the first eminence below the summit of Beinn Ghlas, the view has opened out to the extent that much information about the past and present of the land is laid out in front of you. Down on the southern slope of the hill, dark crescents which were faintly visible from below are now very clear, as are the traces of paths leading up to them. These mark the areas where peat was once cut to provide fuel for the shielings at the bottom of the tracks. Depending on the time of year, you may see other discoloured patches, which mark the selected burning of areas of heather. Even this plant, which to many seems to typify the unspoiled Scottish scene, is carefully controlled, in order to ensure that the right mixture of plants of the right ages is available to provide both feeding and cover for the red

John May on Beinn Ghlas, looking out over the Tay valley. The distinction between the valley pasture and the rough moorland is clearly seen.

grouse, in preparation for the guns of the 'Glorious Twelfth' of August. In fact the whole hill has been adapted by man to meet the various needs of grazing, power supply, shooting, walking and skiing. Each activity has resulted in its own special kind of mark on the landscape before us.

By the time we reach the summit of Beinn Ghlas, 3,657 feet above sea level – higher than any mountain top in England or Wales – an even wider vista has opened up. Looking down on Loch Tay we can see just how narrow a band of green there is between the lake and the beginning of the rough moorland. This is why, with such slender agricultural resources available, the system of transhumance developed. This same point is even more vividly illustrated in a quite literal sense by the valley of the Lyon to the north, where the grassland appears as a patch of startlingly brilliant

The explanation for the dry stream: the dam that enables water to be diverted to the nearby hydroelectric plant.

General Wade's bridge at Aberfeldy.

green among the surrounding hills of rock and heather.

Along the shore of Loch Tay settlements and roads seem squashed into the same thin strip. Roads are themselves comparatively recent intrusions into this landscape. Shieling tracks and drove roads, rather than paved roads, were all that the area could boast until the eighteenth century. The first true road in the modern sense was constructed at the eastern end of Loch Tay, running north to Tummel and east to Aberfeldy. At Aberfeldy an unusually ornate bridge over the Tay bears a plaque telling the passer-by who was responsible for the work. Or, to be more precise, two plaques give the information, one in Latin and one in English. The message, however, is the same: the road was the work of the soldiers led by General Wade. During the Jacobite rebellion of 1745 the lack of roads had hampered the movement of the English troops, so a new system of military roads was introduced to the Highlands to ensure there would be no repetition. This particular road system is not visible from the summit, but it is well to be aware of how recent an addition roads are in this landscape. In earlier times the region was less concerned with communication than with self-sufficiency.

The landscape has changed and is changing. Forestry plantation has resulted in great blocks of dark green being laid on the land, their clean, ruled edges ensuring that no one could mistake them for survivors from the great wild forest.

Those with enough energy left can now follow the ridge to the east to the summit of Ben Lawers itself, where there are more and wider views to be obtained. The return journey is necessarily on the same basic track as that taken up the hill until the burn is regained. The way down is now via the shieling track, but there is a last diversion for those who want to see the whole of the nature trail. Just to the west of the point where the paths meet is a small cliff where many of the alpine plants for which the area is famous can be found. Back at the visitor centre displays show the history of the region we have just walked.

Our mountain landscape has turned out to have a more diverse and varied history than we might have guessed. The next mountain walk will show an even greater diversity.

WALK 2

ANCIENT SETTLEMENTS

Route: *A circular tour of Holyhead Mountain (7 miles)*
Map: *OS Sheet 114 (1:50 000 series)*

In a sense, this route takes us to a level of remoteness even greater than that offered by the Highlands of Scotland, for we are going to an island off an island off the mainland of Wales, to Holy Island, just beyond Anglesey. Yet, paradoxically, this is one of the best known and most often visited corners of Britain. There is a constant stream of traffic to the tiny island for it is, as it has been for many centuries, the point of contact between Ireland and the rest of

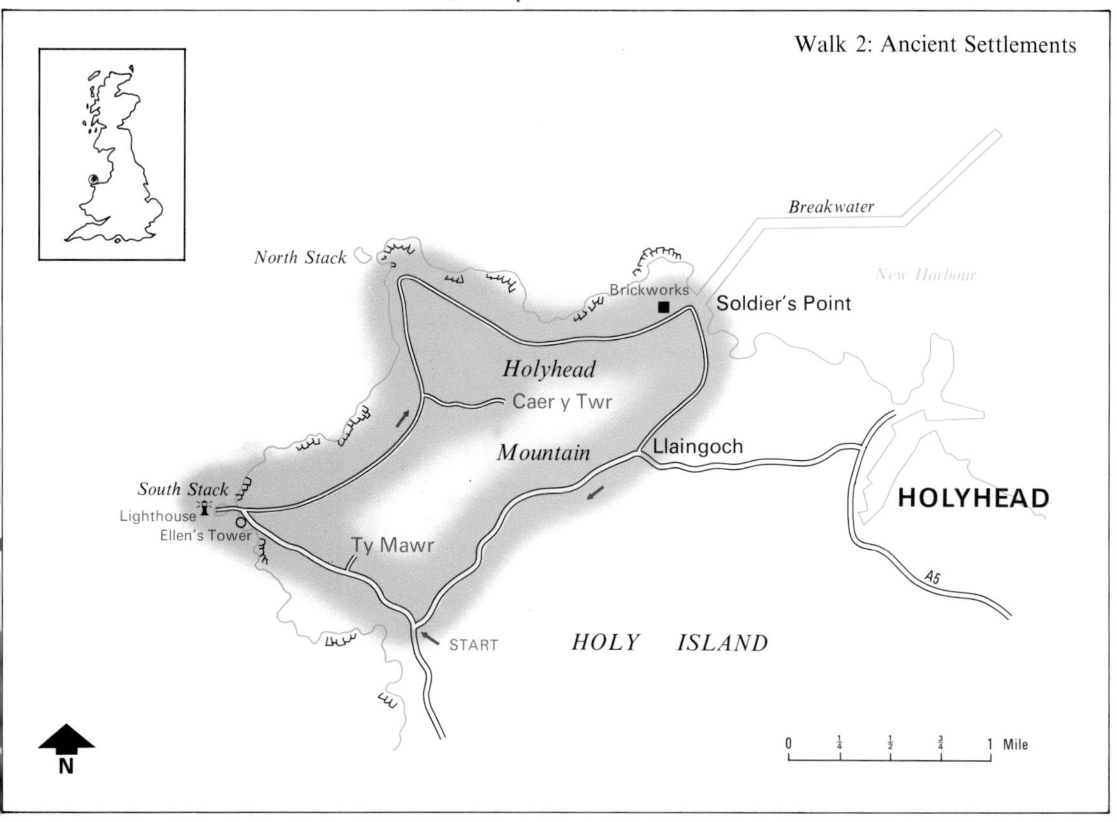

Britain. The importance of this route quickly becomes clear as we approach the island by road from the mainland. The Holyhead road, roughly speaking the modern A5, was vastly improved in the nineteenth century, with whole new sections being constructed, under the supervision of the Scots engineer Thomas Telford. This was to be a major trunk road, which could carry passengers and, more important, the royal mail on the way to and from Ireland. There are many small-scale survivors of those days – milestones, toll-gates remarkably similar in style to the famous 'sunburst' designs of the art deco movement, and toll-houses where passengers paid for the privilege of using the new, improved route. But the strongest possible testimony to the importance of the new road can be seen in Telford's splendid suspension bridge across the Menai Straits. Not very far away, another great engineer, Robert Stephenson, famous son of a famous father, built a second bridge across the straits, a remarkable tubular bridge, to carry the railway to Holyhead. Sadly, this was damaged by fire in 1970, but although its character has changed it remains in use. With its completion, the years of isolation were over. Yet Anglesey remains very much a remote corner of Britain, and very much Celtic Britain at that, for Welsh is still widely spoken on the island. And our walk round Holyhead Mountain will offer a good deal of evidence of the remote Celtic past.

The walk begins on the western side of the mountain, where the minor road past the southern edge turns north-west towards South Stack (map reference SH 217815). Even the most casual glance around the scenery at once suggests two local activities on the island: farming and quarrying. The land is chequered with small fields and the mountain top is a mass of shattered rock. We shall be seeing more of the stone-working trade later on in the walk, so we can start now with a closer look at the landscape of farming. There is nothing here to suggest any great wealth. The farms are remarkably close together, each set in the middle of a group of small fields divided by stone walls. They offer grazing for a few sheep and cattle but nothing else. The mountain is barren and stony, so the farmers here cannot emulate those at Tayside and put their herds and flocks out on the hill for summer pasture. Good farming land is further limited by an area of rough, boggy ground. So, in the circumstances of such small holdings, it is hardly surprising to find that farmhouses are small, built in a plain, vernacular style with little or no attempt at decoration. It is a style of farming that seems to have changed little with the centuries, and the narrow road, scarcely more than a lane running between high grass banks topped by low stone walls, is also suggestive of a long local tradition.

There is, however, another element to the Holyhead story, one of the greatest importance – the surrounding sea. At the entrance to the lane is a stone pillar with an inscription that announces that it was placed there by Trinity House in 1809. Trinity House is a corporation which received a royal charter in 1514 giving it responsibility for the safety of navigation around the British coast – a responsibility it still holds today. In practice, Trinity House today looks after the lighthouses and lightships for England, Wales, the Channel Islands and, rather surprisingly, Gibraltar. It is also the pilotage authority for London and many other coastal districts. So what at first sight looks like a road built to serve local farmers may have a quite different origin, and a row of plain cottages higher up the hill has a uniformity of style that shows that they were built as a unit. Their appearance is in fact very familiar to anyone who has visited the coast and seen cottages for coastguards, lighthouse keepers and all who are concerned with safety at sea. The significance of the dated post and the cottages will be clear shortly, but first we are going to look back far beyond 1809.

Half a mile up the road is a sign pointing off towards the mountain, and announcing the presence of Ty Mawr. At first glance there is little to see except gorse and bracken, but as you wander through you soon find the remains of buildings. There are altogether twenty circular structures built of stone. Today, they only rise for a few courses above ground level, but they have clearly defined entrances and in some you can still just make out the traces of a central hearth. So we are looking at dwellings, and circular dwellings such as this are absolutely typical of early Celtic settlements. These in fact date back to the Iron Age. As well as these circular huts, there are also a few rectangular buildings which are much smaller and which might have been workshops or stores, for they are certainly too small to be houses. Archaeologists did find some evidence of metalworking here, for there were traces of copper slag in one of the huts. Such huts seem to suggest great antiquity, but families were working and living here right through the Roman occupation. It is rather pleasant to conjecture that craftsmen used the locally available copper to make souvenirs for the Roman troops stationed in the town of Holyhead.

Equally conjectural is a theory that led to the local name for this settlement, Cytiau'r Gwyddelod – the huts of the Irish. This is based on the idea that these were houses for the goidels, a group driven out of their Irish homeland by the Brythonic Celts. There is

The remains of the circular huts of Ty Mawr.

no evidence of any sort whatsoever to support that view. What archaeologists have found is evidence of a small self-sufficient community that ground its grain, made pots, spun and wove as well as working in metal. This was an organized settlement living, as the remains still show, in good, solid, well constructed stone houses. Everything suggests a peaceful, rural community – but later in the walk we shall find evidence of another aspect of the life of the period.

From here, retrace your steps to the road and then continue on towards the sea on the footpath marked to Twr Ellin, Ellen's Tower. Seen from a distance, the little castellated building on the cliffs is something of a mystery. It is too small for a fortification. Perhaps it might be a watch-tower or lookout, but why the crenellation? The most likely explanation is that this is a little prospect tower built purely for viewing scenery, given its mock battlements as a touch of whimsy. When we reach the tower, this is just what it proves to be. It was built in 1868 by the Member of Parliament for Pen Rhos, Owen Stanley, as a memorial to his wife Ellen. From here you can follow a clifftop path – with, of course, due care and attention – towards South Stack. The area is now a nature reserve, a splendid place from which to study the local sea-birds which wheel and clamour around the cliffs. Ahead, on its own rocky islet, is the South Stack lighthouse.

The lighthouse stands at the end of the road on which we began our journey and which bore the 1809 stone marker. The lighthouse was completed, and the lantern first lit, on 9 February of that year. Externally, the lighthouse has changed little since it was first built. The circular stone tower is 91 feet high, 22 feet in diameter at the base, tapering to 14 feet at the lantern. At its base are the living quarters, engine-house and stand-by generators, What has changed is the light itself. On quiet days, visitors are admitted to the lighthouse and can see the optical equipment, which weighs over 8 tons but which, floating on a bath of mercury, can be moved by a push of the finger. In order to reach the light, however, you must first get on to the islet and this involves a walk down the cliff steps, all four hundred of them, and, more alarmingly, a walk back up again. It is worth the effort, however, even when the lighthouse is closed to visitors for you get a fine view of the cliffs and some more information about the lighthouse itself.

Only an expert geologist could describe all the rocks of Anglesey and Holyhead with accuracy for there is a great mixture. But here by the cliffs you can look across at the great folds and twists of the face caused by intense pressure and heat, which indicates that they are very ancient, pre-Cambrian rocks. Here, too, you get a splendid view of the sea-birds – the ubiquitous gulls, but also the less common razorbills and guillemots and little puffins popping in and out of holes in the cliff. At the foot of the steps is a

South Stack lighthouse, a self-contained unit on its own islet.

suspension bridge that crosses the 90-foot gap to the islet. It was built in 1828 and before that access to the lighthouse was by a basket slung on a hempen rope. The bridge also acts as a support for the main services of water, power and communications. After seeing all there is to see at South Stack and renegotiating the four hundred steps, you can take a breather and pause to look at the remains of a stone building on the cliff top. There are traces of iron mountings, and it appears to have held some kind of winch. Its position opposite the lighthouse suggests that it may have been part of a cable communication system.

Up here on the cliff top there is ample evidence of Holy Island's importance as a communication centre. The Royal Navy has been here, and there is a merchant navy signal post, identified by the red ensign. At the time of our visit, a British Telecom station was under construction.

At this point the path divides, one branch following on round the cliffs, the second leading uphill – our route to the summit of Holyhead Mountain. To the south, the hill falls away in steep precipices forming natural barriers. But other less natural barriers appear as we begin to explore the jumble of rocks on the summit. The summit itself takes the form of a plateau which slopes away comparatively gently on its northern side. Here a massive wall has been constructed of rocks, quite clearly for defensive purposes. A defensive wall implies that there was something to defend, and it is a reasonable deduction that this was a fortified settlement. These are, in fact, the remains of an Iron Age, hill fort, Caer y Twr, where the inhabitants of Ty Mawr could retreat with their livestock when danger threatened.

The tall chimney surrounded by low kilns that indicate a brickworks.

Today the site of the fort also provides a splendid viewpoint from which virtually the whole of the island can be seen. The most prominent features are those around the town of Holyhead. A huge stone breakwater stretches over a mile out to sea, protecting the New Harbour – new, that is, when it was built in 1873. To the east is the more recently constructed ferry terminal. The inner harbour itself was the work of the famous civil engineer John Rennie, and was completed in 1821. Further to the east, the horizon is dominated by a tall chimney, which marks the aluminium smelting works between Holyhead and Pen Rhos. To the north, the island juts out towards the islet of North Stack, and it is in this direction that our path now leads.

A certain amount of care is needed in descending the steep path down Holyhead mountain. Eventually you will come out by the remains of an old signal station and its modern counterpart set up here on the northern extremity of the island. As at South Stack, there is nothing between this high ground and Ireland except the sea. Now follow the coastal path round to a large quarry and a group of buildings which caused a great deal of puzzlement to the authors. The quarry itself is no problem, for you can see ample evidence of the local building stone being used in the area – not least in the great breakwater seen from the top of the mountain. The puzzle lies in the buildings, though the first group, closest to the quarry face, present few difficulties. Here are substantial stone buildings with cast-iron windows still in place. It is not easy to be more precise about their function if you come here as a casual visitor, as there are 'keep off' notices and council permission is needed for a closer inspection. But even from a distance it is not difficult to make out some form of engine-house and a mechanism for breaking and crushing stone. This form of installation is common at quarries. The next group of buildings comprises a tall chimney and low brick structure containing collapsed domes, also built of brick. Set this down in lowland clay and you have, unmistakably, the kilns of a brickworks. Here the clay would have been shaped and then placed in the heated kilns to harden into brick. Here, though, we are not in the clayey lowlands, but on a stony mountain. What is a brickworks doing here? The clue lies literally underfoot, not in the soil but in the stone and rock. Caught by the sun they sparkle and gleam with pinpoints of light. These reflections come from silica in the rock. The low-grade stone that is useless for building can be crushed and the resulting powder used in the manufacture of fireproof bricks that can be used, for example, as furnace linings. So the first thought, that this was a

The remains of a kiln where fireproof bricks were once made.

brickworks, turns out to be correct after all. A track, level and straight, leads away from the quarry towards the east, and the appearance of sleepers and rusted rails soon confirms that it is an old railway line heading off towards the harbour and breakwater. And it can, in fact, be traced right out along the breakwater itself.

Just before the breakwater is reached a group of castellated buildings appears which, unlike Ellen's Tower, are very definitely of a size to suggest that they are military. Add to this the name of the area – Soldiers' Point – and you can be sure that you have reached the Holyhead garrison. There is further evidence of military activity in the Second World War concrete pillboxes.

It is well worth while walking on to get a closer look at the breakwater to see the impressive scale of the enterprise, the great size of the stone blocks used in its construction and in the construction of the adjoining harbour. This is the focal point of all activity in the island – harbour, ferry terminal and rail terminal are all close at hand and here, as one would expect, is Holy Island's only sizeable town. Those who have the time to make a diversion into Holyhead itself will find evidence that its importance goes back a long way – back indeed to the time of the hut settlements we have already seen on the far side of the mountain. Surrounding the church and churchyard of St Cybi's are walls, with remains of circular towers at three of the four corners. This is the Roman fort, Caer Gybi. Even in Roman times this communication centre merited a military presence.

From the breakwater take the road towards Holyhead and then turn off on a footpath by the bridge. This leads over fields towards Llaingoch. From Llaingoch, follow the minor road round the southern edge of Holyhead Mountain. Again, stone quarries form a prominent feature in the landscape, and their development has involved some very substantial engineering works. The tracks up the hillside are heavily buttressed to give stability and stop possible landslips. The land to the south is wet and marshy, but cut by a prominent drainage ditch. A small octagonal tower stands by the roadside, closed by an imposing iron door. Gurglings of water can be heard inside. Beyond are expanses of water in what are clearly man-made ponds, for alongside the ponds you can still see the mounds of earth dug out during their construction.

This is an intriguing landscape. Here are a large number of clues about land use, but clearly we are looking at the remains of a past activity. Can we put these pieces of evidence together and come up with a plausible solution? If we were seeing this in isolation, it might prove a little difficult, but the presence of brickmaking in the area does lead to some fairly obvious thoughts. The drainage ditch and building clearly belong together and the building can be identified as a pump-house. The pits once yielded clay; now that the pump has ceased to work, they have refilled with water. This sort of deduction can be confirmed by later investigation of documents, as described in 'Following Up Leads'. As far as the walk is concerned, this is the last problem to be solved. It is not, however, quite the end of the interest to be found in the landscape.

Holyhead Mountain with the ramparts of the Iron Age hill fort. Down below is the nineteenth-century breakwater.

To the south is the one exception to the rule about local farms being very small. Pen-y-bonc is an attractive farmhouse with truly massive stone barns attached. A short walk now brings us back to our starting-point.

This has been a comparatively short walk and we have come to one of Britain's extremities to make it, so it would be a shame to return to the mainland without taking time to look at at least two sites which help to reinforce some of the points made in the walk. Anglesey is extraordinarily rich in archaeological sites, but one in particular has particular reference to those we have just seen. Din Lligwy combines our two Iron Age themes into a single location, for here there are both well defined and well preserved huts set within the defensive walls of the hill fort. The site is just north of Llanallgo at SH 496862. Close at hand is a site taking us even further back in time, a giant cromlech, or burial chamber. A ring of stones supports the huge flat stone, 18 feet across at its widest and weighing about 25 tons. It covers an underground chamber where bodies were interred from neolithic times right up to the Bronze Age.

When looking at the huts of Ty Mawr we saw workshops which might well have been used for working copper. In fact, copper mining was to become a major industry on the island. In the eighteenth century it was discovered that Parys Mountain (SH 4490) was virtually one giant chunk of copper ore. It was mined and quarried until it finished up as full of holes as a gruyère cheese. The ore was all removed and the mountain was left bare and desolate with its memories of a mining past. You can still see engine-house and windmill and the great array of settling-beds

A cromlech, or Bronze Age burial mound.

A sterile landscape: the eighteenth-century copper-mining site of Parys Mountain. In the foreground are the settling tanks; behind is the ruined engine house.

where the mineral was extracted. It is a fascinating place in its own right and even today you can still confirm what went on there by rummaging through the spoil heaps to find remnants of greenish copper ore. It provides a very satisfactory conclusion to an outing to think that this same ore was worked within quite modern times – and was also worked by the men of the round huts and the hill forts.

WALK 3

WAR AND PEACE

Route: *A circular walk round Chollerford, Chollerton, Cocklaw and Wall (7 miles). The walk starts at Turret 26B of Hadrian's Wall on the A6079, a quarter of a mile south of the crossroads with the B6318, map reference 919698.*

Map: *OS Sheet 87 (1:50 000 series)*

Hadrian's Wall, which dominates the local landscape, was built two thousand years ago to keep out the marauding Scots. Today, however, as we look across the valley of the North Tyne to Chollerford bridge, everything seems peaceful. This is a deceptive countryside for, as will become evident, there are signs of earlier habitation and other important conflicts as well as more peaceful events, each leaving its mark. After looking at the turret with its worked stone and pondering the reason for the grooves in the doorway (an ill-fitting door gradually scraping away the stone; a drainage channel to keep the floor dry?), return to the road and walk north to the roundabout.

At the roundabout is a modern police house. It has a tall central chimney and functional square windows looking out at all points

The mysterious grooves in the doorway of Turret 26B on Hadrian's Wall.

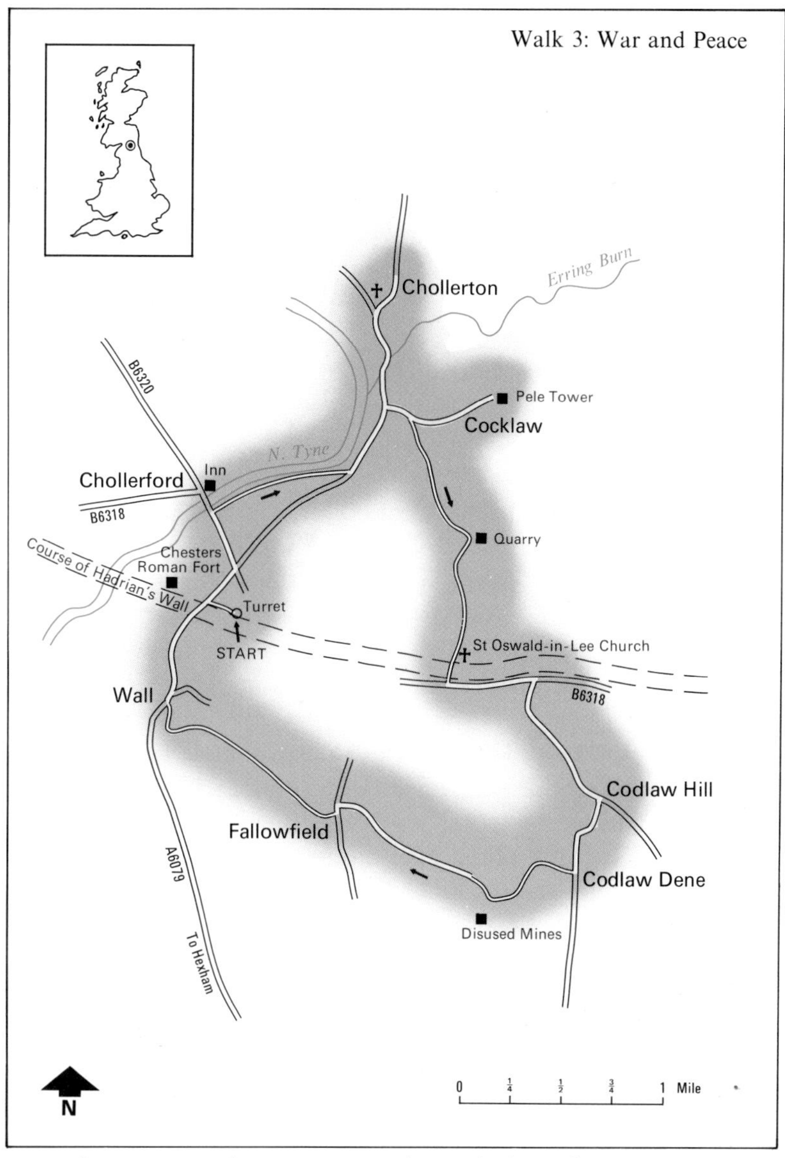

over the surrounding countryside: today's policeman, like the Roman centurion, needs to keep a lookout. From here you can see Chollerford, a utilitarian crossing – just a bridge and an inn, all the traveller needs. Our walk continues down to the bridge and north along the footpath on the east side of the river. However, it is worth mentioning two diversions to look at Roman sites. First, an excursion along a marked footpath on the left of the road to see what remains of the Roman bridge: this is on the line of the wall south of the present bridge, which was built in 1775. The river has changed its course, leaving the eastern abutment of the Roman

The model farm at Chollerford with workers' terrace, barns and windmill. The industrial chimney is an unusual addition.

bridge on dry land. The large stone blocks, carefully dressed, are held together by iron clamps or a complex system of dovetailed joints. Other remains can be seen on the opposite bank and in the water. The second diversion is to Chesters Roman fort. Here there is much to see, not only of the fort itself but also in the museum, built early this century, which houses some fine statues and artefacts.

Close by Chollerford bridge is the railway station, closed in 1956 and like so many others converted into a private dwelling. Despite this, signs of its working days survive in the gas lamps and the still discernible platforms and goods sidings. Can we detect a distinctive North British Railway Company style of architecture? Is it as recognizable a type as, for example, a piece of Great Western Railway architecture? Railway style is a matter of subtlety in proportion and materials and can provide as clear a trademark as the superb North British carriage windows at the Rocking Horse at Hexham, formerly the Railway Hotel. On the other side of the bridge a shallow, sweeping weir provides a constant background of sound.

The footpath starts with steps made from single blocks of stone and progresses between the river and the railway. As so often happens they follow each other through the valley, but on this comparatively low stretch the railway needs an embankment. Soon we reach a stile in the form of a wall with large protruding stones, the first of many built this way – an example of how local materials are used in a very practical manner. The next landmark is a brick bridge carrying the road over the disused railway. It is a skew bridge; that is, the line of the arch is not at right angles to the abutment, allowing the bridge to cross the railway at an oblique angle, a technique first developed in the canal age. The bridge has been given a new lease of life as a shelter for farm machinery. Just beyond the bridge the path rejoins the road by way of a stile. Along the disused railway line which sweeps in front of us various railway relics can be seen – a platelayer's hut, a short platform indicating goods use (it's too short for coaches) and a stone structure set back from the line with its top level with the hill behind. We shall take a closer look at this later.

As we continue north along the road Chollerton comes into view. The main walk is to the right under the railway bridge at NY 932713, but various features now visible towards Chollerton pose a puzzle. There seems to be a tower of some sort in a group of buildings. It looks as though it could be an old windmill but there is something else on the skyline and in the layout of the group which needs investigation, so we continue on this road.

To the right the railway is now on a high embankment leading to a viaduct crossing the road and Erring Burn. Once under the viaduct we can see the buildings in more detail. First is the little church with its lopsided spire and wooden belfry, together with a stable for those using the church. In the church there are some preserved Roman columns in the south arcade and a Roman altar. As so often happens to the landscape detective, tracking down one objective leads to other bonuses. If it were not for the tower on the skyline the church would have been ignored. However, now the tower can be seen. We were correct in thinking that it was once a windmill but close to this dominant feature is a square industrial chimney with, at its base, what seems to be an engine-house. Isolated industrial chimneys are not uncommon but this one, as an integral part of an agricultural unit, seems a puzzle until set in the context of the disused windmill next door. This was an engine for driving a threshing machine. The whole farm complex is carefully planned with the farmhouse, farm buildings and a row of workers' cottages set round a grass triangle by the road – efficient, solid, prosperous and very pleasing to the eye.

Retracing our steps to pick up our original route we take in the view across the valley with the viaduct in the foreground and, to its left, a square stone tower. This is the Cocklaw Tower and our next objective. As we get closer to the tower there are various things to take note of. First, it is an integral part of the farm buildings, but in a different way from the model group in Chollerton. There the cottages, house, engine-house and farm buildings had evolved into a well laid out, almost picturesque, group. Cocklaw is more stark and functional: seen from across the valley it is awesome;

Cocklaw tower is positioned to provide a clear view of the hills from which an attack might have come.

solid with no visible windows or doors. These are at the side with the main entrance high up at first-floor level, and defensible. Cocklaw is a pele tower, built in the fifteenth century. This is the third example of a defence system on the walk. First the Roman, now mellowed in stature by age, surrounded by official notices and its reality blunted by the inability of the imagination to span two thousand years. Second, the police house, almost quaint in its juxtaposition to a modern roundabout. These contrast with the pele tower first seen by the authors through mist and drizzle when it was easy to imagine families barricading themselves against the brutal border raiders from across the valley.

From the main road, our route follows the footpath up the hill marked to St Oswald's Cross. We can put aside thoughts of conflict for a moment and concentrate on the stone structures by the railway line that we glimpsed earlier. At first glance they look like hoppers for loading, but they are too far from the railway line. Besides, what would they load? Obviously some process took place between the top of the structure and the railway itself. A track leads away from this point and farther up the hill we find deep recesses and curved mounds in the landscape, definite signs of man's shaping as opposed to natural evolution – in fact quarrying. This is a limestone region and it is a fair assumption that we have come across an area for the production of lime. As farming became more intensive and more geared to cereal production, there was more need to combat the acidity of the soil by enriching it. Limestone was quarried and transported to a kiln, usually situated close to a means of transport as a quarry supplied more stone than was needed in the immediate locality. The kiln was basically a brick-lined tube into which the limestone was tipped, layered with coal and burnt. This layering ensured a continuous process and the lime was removed from the bottom of the kiln and loaded for distribution.

At the top of the hill there are large spoil heaps, the residue of quarrying, complete with pieces of limestone, which adds force to our theory. Looking back down the hill there is an unusual aspect to the land pattern. The hillside has been worked to provide an even slope from the top, with its signs of quarrying, to the upper

This brake drum was an important clue that led to the discovery of an inclined plane.

A cross-section view of the quarry at the top of the inclined plane. The different strata show up clearly.

part of the kilns by the railway line below. Further up there are more signs of man-made bumps and also a change from the lush grass of the hillside to a more struggling vegetation on the spoil heaps. As we cross the stile a building comes into view – the remains of a shed housing a large round drum with a handle projecting from it, still with the remains of a brake block. There are railway sleepers and a second shed. In this there is a stone floor, a roller over which a hawser might have been passed and a large stone block with signs of an engine mounting. From the top of the levelled path we can see a line of sleepers leading towards the lime kilns, and even a length of cable in the bushes – all the signs of an inclined plane, up and down which trucks could be hauled by cable.

Past the sheds and round a bend the quarry comes into view. It is gigantic. There is a good cross-section view of the workings of the quarry. A good fifteen to twenty feet of loose material had to be removed before the first limestone layer was reached. The face of the quarry is a vertical wall sixty feet high. At its foot there are more clues – a pulley in a bush, rails and sleepers in the grass. The layout of the floor of the quarry shows how much work was put into making the internal transport system. Even where there are no rails or sleepers it is possible to see where the tracks had been laid. The lines circle the quarry floor and stretch right up to the working face, where they reach their highest point. Thus the trucks made their upward journey empty and the return trip, loaded, was aided by gravity.

From the end of the quarry the footpath continues to the brow of the hill. In the distance is a large barn-like building set in isolation with a familiar but as yet unrecognizable air. The path changes its character from a rough track to a definite worked causeway. It is raised above the level of the fields and is bounded on one side by very mature trees. On the left, by contrast, is a later path with smooth curves and inclines which leads to more workings. Clearly it is not part of the older causeway. Also to the left there is a glimpse of another pele tower.

However, the focus of our attention is the barn-like building. It appears to be buttressed and it has a small belfry and a sundial. This is the church of St Oswald-in-Lee and marks the place of another time of strife, for, according to St Bede, it was here in AD 635 that the Christian St Oswald, having erected a stone cross virtually single-handed, defeated the heathen Cadwalla and his superior forces, establishing the foundations of Christianity in Northumbria. In the porch above the door is part of a stone cross with a carved figure on it. The inside of the church, which was built in 1737 to replace an earlier one, is impressive in its simplicity and includes ancient stonework in the north wall. Inside is a splendid, ornate harmonium. Was the first half of the eighteenth century a particularly prosperous time for this area, with the church and bridge both built at that time? Down the church path by the road stands a modern cross made of wood, marking the site of the old stone one. The field now dips along its entire length parallel to the road. The dip is too even and sudden to be natural – we have rejoined Hadrian's Wall for the first time since the start of our walk. The ditch is an integral part of the wall's design, confronting an enemy approaching from the north with a double obstacle.

At the road our route turns east. On each side there are earthworks, suggesting that the road follows the top of the wall. The walls of a farm building on our left include several large dressed stones – more a sign of economy than an architectural feature. After the farm the remains of Hadrian's Wall are much more pronounced. The scale of the work makes you wonder how many engineering breakthroughs were accomplished in devising systems for what now seems the most obvious of tasks.

At the signpost to Codlaw Hill we turn south. On our left is a puzzle – a large enclosed area adjacent to the Roman wall. There is an obvious boundary, with the remains of an older stone wall inside the present drystone one and of a totally different nature. The field contains lumps and bumps with large stones and a sprinkling of gorse bushes, which may indicate a different soil structure. The road follows the boundary, which suggests that it is an ancient track. However, there is nothing on the Ordnance

Survey map to help us so this discovery must await later research.

This is a good part of the walk to look around and ponder the landscape. It is open and mainly barren, with heathers, grassland and sheep. There is a small hollow with signs of moorland grass, indicating a bog. The trees are drastically bent by the prevailing wind and everything seems to be in isolated huddles; buildings and trees are clustered for protection, much as the sheep huddle in the wind. Each farm belongs to its immediate environment, giving an air of self-sufficiency. South of Codlaw Hill, the road is gated, for here sheep take precedence over motorists.

At Codlaw Dene we take a footpath to the right (map reference 945682), passing close to the farmhouse with a copse on the immediate left. A small bridge carries the path across a stream and into a wood. There are immediate signs of workings and a small clearing with some holes in the ground, and a track leading down to more lime kilns on the right.

Further on there are more clues to an industrial past. Once again the path has the feel of industrial use, smooth in incline and curving, the natural stream following by its side until it disappears to the left. Looking closely, we can see signs of brickwork as the stream passes under the path and through ever better built

A group of small lime kilns.

culverts; at one stage there are sets on the stream bed. Suddenly the area opens up and quite unexpectedly we arrive at another exploring-ground. As before, stop and look first and then explore systematically. On the left is a built-up working with a chute for pouring materials down and a set of steps up to the top. There are signs of ore and in the bushes to the right is a bricked-up hole in the side of the valley. Here is an adit, or horizontal mine entrance. In fact later research revealed it to be a lead mine. Up the steps by the chute there are levels with blocks of stone and a fenced hole, which could be a shaft. At the top there are loading bays for transferring the ore to some means of transport which ran along the top of the valley.

However, our route follows the footpath to Fallowfield. The path climbs steadily and from the higher ground we can see clearly how man has made use of the contours of landscape. At the foot of the valley flows the river and higher up, on a parallel course, are the road and the railway – far enough below the summit to be sheltered. Where the valleys of North Tyne and South Tyne converge, so does everything else and a meeting-point is established, the river is bridged and a settlement is built up and defended. In fact the outskirts of Hexham can be clearly seen.

A splendid cast-iron sign announces Fallowfield Farm, another single settlement but rather grander than those we have seen so far. Surprisingly, perhaps, there is no sign of where the mine workers lived, but it was not unusual to have a few miles to walk to work. The path is signposted to Wall and turns right before the end of a wide stone-walled track. Again the path crosses grazing land and skirts small woods until the promontory above Wall is reached. The village is laid out below. Before descending, look for the signs of an earlier habitation – a cluster of stone circles with hollows and entrances, less clear than at Holyhead but still definitely marking a Celtic settlement, in fact quite a sizeable one. It is interesting to contrast the needs of growing Hexham, in its low, artificially defended position, with the earlier civilizations, which kept to the high ground for natural defence.

The descent to the village of Wall – named, of course, after Hadrian's Wall – is down a flight of slippery single stone steps leading to a village green with its war memorial cross, pump and two churches of different denominations. There is a friendly post office, the size of a garden shed, though heavily barricaded. On one side of the green is a garage with, in summer, a colourful display of flowers planted in beds bordered by green-painted tractor tyres. At its side is a square chimney, which suggests that the garage was once a smithy – a common progression in villages as the internal combustion engine took over from the horse. As we turn right on the main road to return to our starting-point we pass a milestone and a modern feature of the landscape – a lay-by, formed by the straightening of the road, complete with its litter basket surrounded by litter.

The most striking feature of this walk is the changing fortunes of the area. The cluster of Celtic settlements were overshadowed by the national importance of Hadrian's Wall. With the departure of the Romans the area was reduced to individually defended smallholdings again, as seen in the pele tower. The mines and quarrying once again gave the area a wider relevance. Then they were exhausted. The railway came and went, the car now takes precedence, and, once again, only the smallholdings are left. Perhaps this is an indication of the true nature of the landscape, with man's intrusions bringing at best a temporary prosperity.

WALK 4

Forest Trails

Route: *Circular walk through the Forest of Dean, starting at Soudley on the B4227*

Map: *OS Sheet 162 (1:50 000 series)*

This is a walk through the ancient Forest of Dean, a huge area of woodland that fills much of the triangle of land between the rivers Wye and Severn. It is a popular place with visitors, many of whom come because it seems to be a rare example of an 'unspoiled' natural wood, a contrast to the regimented pines of modern forestry. It is a place to find peace and quiet, a refuge from the modern, industrial world. In the course of the walk we shall be seeing just how natural the wood really is and how far removed from industry. We begin at the Dean Heritage Museum between Upper and Lower Soudley (map reference 664107). Those who cannot contain their impatience can go straight into the museum and have many of the questions about the nature of the forest answered; the rest should be content for the time being to look at the building itself, its immediate surroundings – and the map.

Not very much in the way of detective work is needed to recognize the main building for what it is. The Soudley Brook has been dammed, diverted down an artificial channel, or leat, and the water held back behind a massive stone wall to create a pond. Water from the pond is controlled by sluices, so that it can be returned to the stream directly or passed through the building area. This is the standard arrangement of a millpond providing a head of water to drive a water-wheel. It is not perhaps immediately apparent just what machinery the water-wheel drove, and this is not surprising for once you have a water-wheel turning a shaft you can put belts and pulleys on that shaft and drive practically anything. The mill itself with its regular windows and formal facade looks very much what it is, a building of the late nineteenth century. It was in fact built in 1876. What went on there? The first thought when looking at a water mill is of the grinding of corn, and that is exactly what this mill was used for in the early years. Later it was converted for making leatherboard and after that it became a sawmill. Such is the versatility of water power – and such too is the difficulty of determining the nature of this kind of building. At the time of our visit the museum authorities were excavating the area below the mill to reveal the pits where two water-wheels once turned and uncover the tunnel that took the water back down to the stream – the tail-race. The same excavations also revealed great lumps of cinder and darkish chunks of slag.

The museum authorities have begun recreating part of the old life of the forest. In the woods beyond the stream, you can see a curious sort of wigwam, consisting of a framework of branches covered over with brushwood to form a rough shelter. Beside it are carefully stacked piles of logs or logs covered in mud or even a smouldering heap – for this is charcoal burning and what you see depends on what stage the process has reached. Charcoal is simply partially burnt wood, wood that has been left to smoulder but never permitted to burst into flames. The logs are all of even size and are carefully arranged to form a pyramid-like structure which is then packed with earth so that once the fire is lit the air supply can be carefully controlled. It was common practice to work in the forest where the heavy wood was on hand and only the light charcoal needed to be carted away. And, as the process was long,

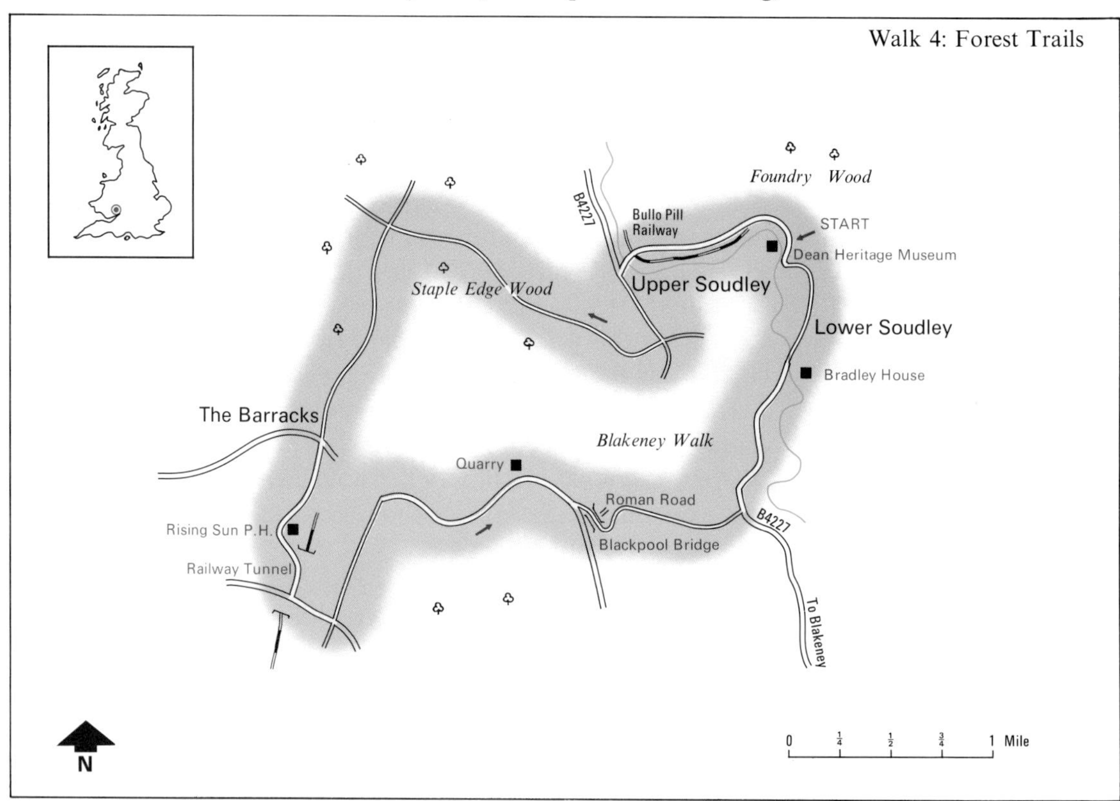

A charcoal burner's shelter with a wood stack ready for burning.

slow and needed constant attention, the charcoal burners lived on the site – hence the wigwam.

Leave the museum and cross the road. Opposite the mill, a wall bears signs of charring – not much evidence of anything other than intense heat, but we later discovered that the wall had once been part of a blacksmith's forge. Walk along the road as it curves round towards the west and look down into the valley of Soudley Brook, where you will see an old, humpbacked bridge across the stream and a trackway, all on a scale that suggests some importance. This was originally the main road in the valley. To the north of the present main road is a large pond with raised banks, suggesting it was man-made, a theory reinforced by its regular shape, narrow at the north and ending in a straight wall of a dam at the south. Our first millpond is not, it seems, the only one in the area. A non-agricultural region such as this would scarcely have needed two grain mills, so what exactly is going on here? A look at the map provides the answer, for the local woodland is Foundry Wood. The equation is complete. Foundry suggests iron, we have woods for charcoal and a check on the local geology shows ironstone deposits. Now ironstone contains oxide of iron and to get the metal it is necessary to get rid of the oxygen by burning. This requires a carbon fuel, but one without impurities, and until the eighteenth century that meant charcoal. Here all the elements literally came together and blast-furnaces were built and foundries established. To work the iron, it needed to be heated and then pounded into shape under massive hammers powered by water – and this explains the ponds. You will find many of these distinctive 'hammer ponds' in woodland areas such as Dean and the Weald of Kent. The one before us is probably the site of the King's Forge, one of four furnace and forge sites established in the forest by James I. Already our natural woodland is appearing as a major industrial area with a long history of ironworking.

Industry needs transport, and to the south the mouth of a tunnel suggests the presence of a railway. Across the road we soon find the platform with its stone coping and a track bed running parallel with the road. So there is an iron industry and a railway to serve it, but it is a very old iron industry and one might wonder about the age of the railway itself. There are signs of stone in the track but nothing to lead us to any definite conclusions until we reach a point where the track is buttressed by a stone wall. Early railways or tramways relied on horses to pull the trucks. Conventional railway sleepers would have been useless for the horse would have tripped over them. So the rails were spiked into parallel rows of square stone blocks. Now just suppose that there was a tramway here, later converted to a conventional railway. The stone blocks would have been dug up and would have been used to reinforce the embankment for the new steam railway. Look at the embankment and you will see square coping blocks, drilled with holes and with a rectangle carved out to hold the iron rail support: splendid confirmation of a theory. This is part of the Bullo Pill Railway from Cinderford to Bullo on the Severn, begun as a tramway in 1809 and converted in 1854. It crosses the road to swing north through a

A squared stone with the distinctive hole that shows it was once a sleeper block for an early tramway.

rock cutting; we, however, continue a little further down the road.

On the right is a farm on top of a knoll. In such a heavily wooded area one might have expected timber buildings but, as the cutting reveals, the forest rests on a base of sandstone, and that is the material used in these solid, uncompromising buildings – irregular, uncoursed blocks of the local stone. The main road now turns north, but we take the minor road to the south to begin our walk through the forest itself. What becomes very quickly clear is that the forest is not uniform. You would not expect to find it limited to one species of tree, but you might expect a fairly regular mix. In fact there are patches where one species dominates or even monopolizes a large area. In the case of the carefully spaced conifers it is not difficult to see the hand of forestry management, for we have all become used to the modern plantation. But other tree patterns also begin to emerge, suggesting that such management might not, after all, be such a very modern phenomenon.

After half a mile, take the wide track that leads off to the right and follow the green pathway to the west. It is very easy to lose your way among these forest tracks so a good map and compass are essential. The track to follow rises steeply towards Staple Edge Wood. Among the trees you will see sweet chestnuts with their massive trunks, large glossy leaves with saw-tooth edge and, in season, the nuts in their spiky outer cases. This is not a native English tree but comes from southern Europe, where the nut is used for both human and animal food. It first came to this country with the Romans, which leads to one or two interesting thoughts about just how long man has been involved in controlling this woodland area. As we climb, the views become ever wider, across a roof of trees down to the Severn to the south and a seemingly endless prospect of woodland to the east and north. The extent is impressive, but the blocks of colour in varying shades of green again emphasize a forest divided into definite areas. Observation closer at hand, throughout the walk, provides firm evidence of man's interference with the natural world.

Among the densely packed conifers are areas of coppicing. Alder, ash, wych-elm and lime are among the trees suitable for this form of cultivation. Coppice is easily recognized. At ground level you can see the wide stump or stool bearing the marks and scars of cutting. From it spring the vertical poles which, in a managed woodland, are regularly harvested so that the whole process can start again. As long as there is life in a tree it will continue to send up new shoots from the mutilated stool. Whatever its age, the coppice can never be mistaken for a natural growth. How was coppicing controlled? Who decided which bit of forest belonged to whom and who had the right to it? You can see evidence of boundaries that indicate ownership. These appear as bank and ditch marking off one part of the forest from another.

The regular spacing of these oaks indicates a positive policy for the development of the forest.

If there is one tree with which Dean is particularly associated it is the English oak, and there are plenty to be seen on our walk, though there are heavier concentrations in other parts of the forest. Again we see signs of regular plantation rather than the haphazard patterns of nature left to her own devices. Inevitably oak inspires thoughts of great ships – heart of oak – and oak did indeed lie at the heart of the wooden ship. To understand the importance of oak you have to think a bit about ship construction and then look at the growth pattern of the tree. In particular, consider not the outer planking of the ship but the massive frame to which the planks are attached. How could horizontal decking be fixed to the vertical walls without the use of metal brackets? The answer is a piece of timber bent in a right angle, but to have the necessary strength the grain of the wood must run true throughout. Such a piece can be cut from the intersection of a wide horizontal branch leaving a broad tree trunk. And which tree grows in precisely this way? The oak. These particular structural members were known as 'knees' and there are 438 of them in HMS *Victory*. That is an awful lot of oak. To meet this huge requirement of timber for the Navy, over 10,000 acres of the Forest of Dean were enclosed and planted with oak at the end of the seventeenth century.

At the top of the ridge we come to an area of wet wasteland. Here, where the soil is thin and the rock pokes through, there is a clearing free of trees and scattered with small ponds. Beyond this is Staple Edge Lodge, a pair of houses which lie in the heart of the wood and can only have been built for use by foresters. Continue on until you reach a 'crossroads' (640105), then take the wide grassy track to the south. As you begin to move steadily downhill keep glancing over to the right and you will see a great hump rising out above the trees, its shape suspiciously unnatural. Its significance will become clear later. Then on your right you will see the two stretches of water of Mallards Pike Lake, which show the same characteristic shape and sluices as we have already seen at Soudley, suggesting a similar function. Cross over between the two lakes and continue on down the path from the car park to the road. Just before the road you cross a broad track which does not merely follow the lie of the land as our walkways have done but is kept on a level by means of cutting and embankment – in short,

An unlikely group of houses for the centre of a forest: these terraces are miners' houses, known as the Barracks.

another railway, which alerts us to look out for more industrial activity in the area.

On reaching the road turn right and at the crossroads you will see a most interesting collection of buildings. A terrace of houses, each with a long allotment-like garden, stretches along the road. They were clearly all built as a piece and are typical of industrial housing. The ground round about is much disturbed and, if you poke among the heaps, pieces of coal can be seen. We have reached a small mining village. Those who want actual confirmation of the nature of the very large hill seen in the wood can walk past the houses, known as the Barracks, take the road to the north and inspect the hill, which turns out indeed to be a colliery spoil heap. Others may prefer to take their deduction on trust and turn south along the road past the ruins of the miners' chapel and head for the Rising Sun pub. This is more than just a pleasant spot to stop and slake one's thirst. It too sits in the middle of spoil heaps. As you go inside pause to look at the emblem engraved in the glass door. It shows a man in medieval costume wielding a short pickaxe – the symbol of the Free Miners of Dean who, by ancient right, are still free to dig for coal and minerals in the forest. A few small, privately worked coal mines survive in the area.

Leaving the pub, follow the road south, noticing the cutting and tunnel entrance at the roadside – yet another railway. At the road junction you will see in the trees in front of you a stumpy circular tower. Immediately beyond it the land falls away steeply and a series of steps leads down to the far end of the tunnel we saw by the road. The tower lies on the tunnel line, and must mark a shaft used originally for hauling out spoil from the excavations and then retained for ventilation. The tunnel itself is securely bricked in. The railway began as a tramway in 1809, the Severn and Wye Railway, and was later converted to a conventional railway. Turn back north again on the forest track paralleling the road you have just come down and join the east–west road near Mallards Pike Lake. Once again we find disturbed ground and foundations of buildings, and this time convincing evidence of what went on here is provided by a circular hollow in the ground, its edges defined by brick – clearly a mine shaft.

Follow the road to the east and note the way the brook has been contained within walls to prevent earth slip and keep it free-running. This is the stream we saw leaving the lake. To the north of the road is another Dean industry of which we received hints at the beginning of the walk – stone quarries. The stone in this area is of good quality and, as well as being used locally, it can be seen in a

Buried among the trees is this bridge that once carried a branch line of the Great Western Railway.

variety of major buildings, from Berkeley power station in the Severn valley to University College, London. Opposite the quarries, just past a sharp bend in the road, look out on the south side for a metal post with a round head. Cast into the top are the initials G.W.R. and the date 1907 – the initials are well enough known and this is, in fact, a boundary post. But where is the railway? Signs soon appear – sleepers used in fencing, rails as posts. It seems an unlikely setting for a part of the Great Western Railway but there it is. Another spoil heap and more signs of building indicate another abandoned mine, behind which is the branch line itself that served the colliery. The main line through the area soon appears in more definite form.

A road junction appears and the road to the north is crossed by a tall railway bridge. This little corner is full of interest. There is a carefully planted avenue of oaks, the railway – and one of the forest's most interesting historical remains. Go under the railway arch, and a secondary roadway can be seen leaving the line of the

The emblem of the Free Miners of Dean, engraved in the glass door of the Rising Sun pub.

main road, its edges marked by vertical kerbstones. It becomes more distinct, with signs of paving stones clearly showing at the surface as it heads off to a fording-point on the stream. This is a remnant of the Roman road that linked iron mines at Lydney to the smelting furnaces at Ariconium, near Weston-under-Penyard. The modern road crosses the stream by a bridge, leaving the route to the ford undisturbed. Cross Blackpool Bridge and take the track to the east across to Ayleford.

This forest walk shows many of the features we have already seen, including one old coppice with poles growing from very large stools. At the houses that mark the edge of the village take the path that runs down the hill to the main Blakeney–Soudley Road. Turn north back towards Soudley but turn off after three-quarters of a mile on to the track that runs down beside a large white house, with a GPO post-box outside. The house stands on a platform high above a stream, and the bank is supported by tall, buttressed walls. The scale of building seems too grand for mere domestic purposes. After what we have already seen, industrial use inevitably comes to mind and the ground provides a clue. There you will see large pieces of fused slag which, together with the name Forge Grove, indicate that this was a forge site. This was Bradley Forge, the house still being known as Bradley House. Follow the bridle path above the stream – a suspiciously flat and level way, carved out of the hillside. By now you should instantly guess that you have reached another tramway. It leads on to a field where, built into the hillside, is another very large and impressive

The remains of the Roman road, leading down to a ford.

A lump of slag found by the stream at Forge Grove.

stone wall. There is not quite enough to identify the structure with certainty, but in the context of this area it seems likely to have some connection with the iron industry. This is all that remains of a blast-furnace site with a record of ironmaking that goes back to the seventeenth century and possibly even earlier. Beside it, near the track, is yet another railway tunnel. It is not particularly impressive to look at but has more than a passing historical interest, for it is arguably the oldest railway tunnel in the world, built in 1809.

The track brings us back to the main road near our starting-point, and provides a good view of the tunnel and the tail-race from the mill. It marks the end of a forest trail which turned out to be an exploration in industrial history.

WALK 5 A FIELD STUDY

Route: *Newbold-on-Avon, Little Lawford, Harborough Magna, Cosford, Newbold-on-Avon ($6\frac{1}{2}$ miles)*

Map: *OS Sheet 140 (1:50 000 series)*

A first glance at the Ordnance Survey map shows a region that seems to be dominated by transport routes, not too surprising for an area close to the heart of England. To the west is the long straight line of the Roman Fosse Way, while more modern roads all but enclose the area where we are to walk – the M6 to the north, M1 to the east and M45 to the south. Railways, too, have a prominent part to play, radiating out from Rugby to all points of the compass; some as still busy main line routes, others, including the once mighty Great Central line, now derelict. It might seem that there is little space left amid all this rush of traffic for the quieter pleasures of the countryside, but a closer look shows a steadily undulating landscape and we shall find it to be rich agricultural land, which still carries clear evidence of the changing pattern of farming over many centuries. Transport and agriculture will be the two themes of this walk, and we shall start with the former.

Travelling out along the B4112 from Rugby, it is not easy to see where Rugby ends and Newbold-on-Avon begins, for the housing has spread out along the road to join the two together. Then you see a pub sign for the Boat Inn and the picture on the sign, showing a canal boat, is a broad enough hint as to what you might expect to find close at hand. Not so many years ago, the sign was somewhat more bewildering, for it showed a square-rigged ship apparently beating round Cape Horn in a gale. This baffled many passers-by for here we are about as far from the sea as you can get in Britain. In fact pub names such as 'ship', 'boat' and those with maritime connections such as 'Lord Nelson' are often an indication, when they appear miles from the sea or a major river, that a canal is close by. So it proves here, and this is the starting-point for the walk. A short length of roadway leads beside the pub and, rather surprisingly, a second pub next door to the canal. This is the

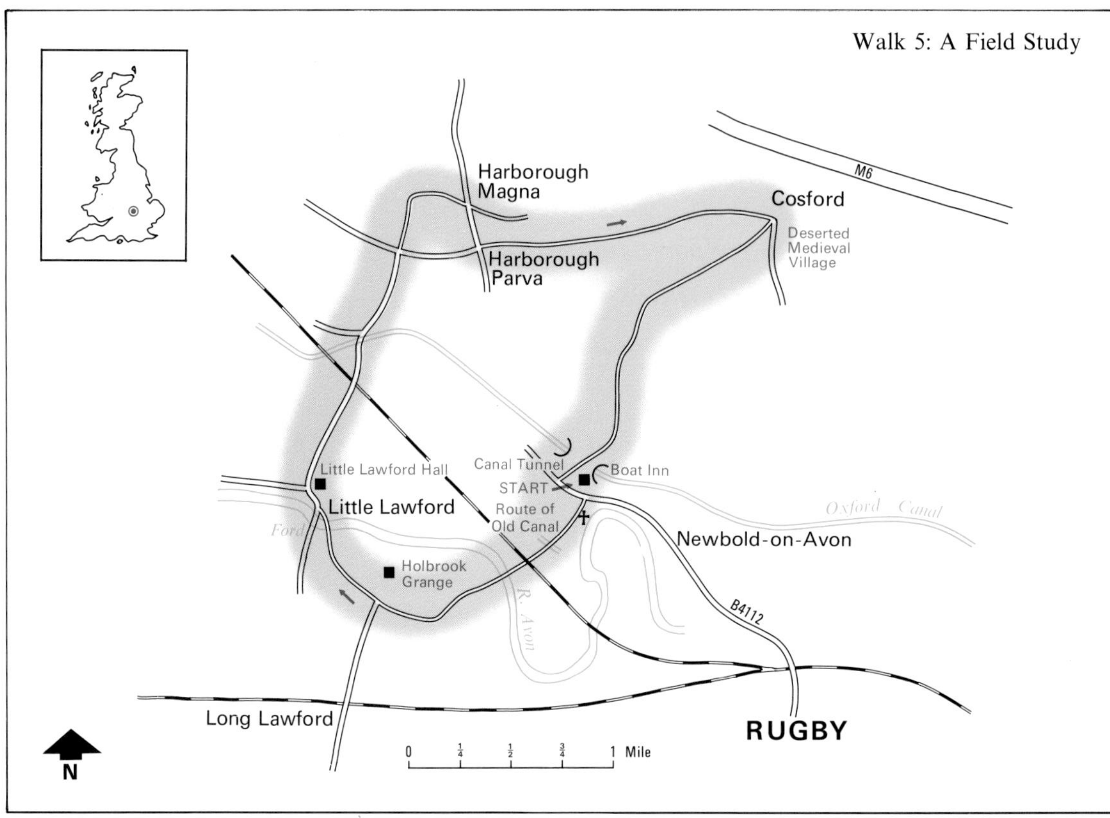

northern section of the Oxford Canal, and you can see at once how the meeting-place of road and canal gave this spot its importance. There is an extensive wharf area, with mooring rings set into the stone, and a small warehouse where goods could be stored awaiting transhipment between cart and boat. And, of course, the pubs, which would have relied on the boat people for much of their trade. Note by the way that this is a narrow canal. This does not mean that the distance between the banks is not very great, but that it has narrow locks, able to take a vessel 72 feet long by 7 feet wide. These are narrow boats, the traditional trading craft of the Midland canals; they are not barges, a word reserved for wide-beamed craft, and they are manned by boatmen, not bargees.

However, to return to the buildings. The most interesting is the warehouse, now converted into a private house. Because trade has ended on the Oxford Canal, and the pleasure boat has taken over from the working boat, we tend to forget that the canals were once hugely important, and centres of innovation. This little building is very much a creature of the Industrial Revolution, making use of the latest ideas in cheap construction. Look, for example, at the windows, where the hexagonally patterned glazing bars are in fact cast iron. Similar windows were produced on a large scale and can be seen on many early industrial buildings. Elsewhere, however, we are very much with the traditional materials of the area – red brick predominating. Look, for example, at the typical humpback bridge, and the rich mixture of colours of the brickwork. These are not the mass-produced bricks of the twentieth century, but bricks burned using local clay in local kilns. As firing was then a somewhat haphazard process, there were considerable colour variations. This is true of the bricks used for all the older structures of the region, and it is this that gives them much of their charm.

Standing here, we can see the canal heading east, after which it will turn south to Oxford, and west towards a junction with the Coventry Canal, but before it reaches that junction it disappears into the short Newbold tunnel. That might seem to be all we can say about the canal, a quiet, unobtrusive feature in the landscape, which still carries clues to its former importance. But there is more to it than that. Walk back to the main road and cross over to the

A cast-iron window, indicating industrial use, beside the Oxford Canal.

church. Although the predominant building material of the area is brick, it is usual for churches and other important buildings to be dignified by stone, and this rather handsome church is no exception. Take the signposted footpath out of the churchyard, and you will see the way ahead marked by an avenue of trees. But first, turn back towards the church, and you will see a semicircular opening on the hillside, and a very clear trough-like indentation in the ground, leading away from it. It looks very like the tunnel entrance back on the canal, and the trough has the right proportions to suggest a filled-in canal. In fact, this is also the Oxford Canal, and this is also the Newbold tunnel. Some explanation should make all clear.

The line of the Oxford Canal was laid down by the great engineer James Brindley, and work was begun in 1769. Brindley's preferred technique when presented with undulating countryside was to take his canal round obstacles rather than through them or over them – this 412-foot-long tunnel was an exception to the general rule. He would travel the country by horseback, eyeing the ground, fixing the line of the canal to follow the natural contours. It is an interesting exercise to try to see the country through his eyes, seeing how one could fit a canal which has to remain on the level on to this uneven ground. Brindley's line is still quite distinct, running in a great sweeping arc south from the church and eventually turning north again. This old route did well enough for a time but the completion of the Grand Junction (now the Grand Union) Canal at the beginning of the nineteenth century brought fresh traffic to the northern end of the Oxford Canal. In the 1820s it was felt that the old meandering canal could no longer cope and it was decided to build a new, straighter line. The plans were made by Marc Brunel, famous father of an even more famous son, and it

The old canal tunnel beside the church at Newbold-on-Avon.

is this new line which is used today. The curves of the old Brindley canal remained as a series of loops off the new main line, but eventually fell into disuse. As you continue your walk down the avenue of trees you will come across the line again, with the remains of a wharf and a typical canal bridge forlorn among the fields.

The canals were the first new transport routes of any significance that Britain had seen since the end of the Roman occupation, and here you can see the two generations together – the wandering, contour-hugging line of the old canal and the bold straight lines of the new. Techniques pioneered here were to be used to great effect by the next generation of engineers, the railway builders. Old and new canal are both unobtrusive features in the landscape; the railway ahead of us looms large on its high embankment, a much more prominent feature. It is worth pausing for a moment to think of the effort that went into building such massive earthworks before the days of earth-shifting machinery. This was the work of men using pickaxe, shovel and barrow.

Beyond the railway a small, but not inelegant, bridge takes you over the Avon and into a different form of landscape. In fact, two quite distinct patterns appear on the face of the land. One is a pattern with which you will become very familiar during this walk of steady undulations like a vast corrugated sheet – the distinctive mark of ridge and furrow that here denotes a medieval field. We shall be looking at that in rather more detail further on in the walk, where it forms part of an important story of the changing landscape. The other pattern we can see is of broad expanses of grassland, dotted with strategically placed trees. One might look at this and think of it as being a fine example of a very natural, very English landscape. But it is so well ordered that it is clearly an artificial creation. What we are seeing is the parkland of the great house, Holbrook Grange. It is an idealized landscape based on the well-known principles laid down in the eighteenth century by Capability Brown and the other great landscape gardeners. It is a landscape designed not for use, but to be admired. Over on the left you can see the working part of the estate, the handsome, well ordered Home Farm. There is a fine air of tranquillity about this scene of great house, park and farm and much care and thought has gone into its creation. Note that even the little bridge carrying the driveway across a stream is an elegant structure of stone and in the distance you can see an even finer wooden footbridge. Only the distant chimneys of the cement works at Rugby remind you of the modern world.

The elegant cast-iron bridge still bears the name of the maker, Horseley Ironworks.

The path leads to the edge of a modern housing estate and you emerge briefly into the street before taking the path out again which, at the time of writing, appears as a gap beside a bright pink wall. The way now heads north-west through the park back to the Avon again, which is crossed by a bridge with a raised footpath to carry it above flood level. Upstream, a weir has been built across the river and obviously it was built to serve a purpose. It acts as a dam ensuring deep water upstream, some of which can be seen entering an artificial channel, or leat, running away from the river. That water was intended to be used for power, and in this agricultural district you would expect that power to be used to work the machinery of a grain mill. So the sight of the weir leads you to expect a mill, and that is just what you find as you cross the river into Little Lawford – a rather splendid mill with attached mill house. The mill is easily identified by a shaft end protruding through the gable wall and the remains of sack hoists. The water-wheel has gone but the wheel pit can be seen where the water rushes under two arches, the one nearest the mill being lined with stone sets.

Walk past the mill and turn left and you reach the spot where mill-stream and river reunite. Here the river is fordable – though it is as well to check the measuring post at the river's edge before venturing into the water. The wall beside the ford is built in the distinctive red sandstone found in this part of the world. It is an attractive stone but does not weather well, hence the wide use of brick for building.

Little Lawford has one surprise in store, the old hall. This conforms to the rule that if a building is of sufficient importance stone will be brought in from other areas for its construction. This magnificent house, dated 1694 above the central doorway, is built of coursed rubble in a most unusual style. The dripstone mouldings seem very appropriate to the rough walls, but they stand above very unusual pointed Gothic windows. Altogether this is a decidedly attractive house but a very eccentric one. It is interesting to note that already in our short walk we have come across two grand houses, a measure of the wealth of the district, based very much on the rich fertility of the soil.

The next stage follows the minor road that leads northwards to Harborough Magna. The landscape is again primarily agricultural, fields divided between pasture and arable. There is every indication that this is a long-established route for, mercifully, this is an area where old hedgerows have not been grubbed out to be replaced by the anonymity of the wire fence. So as you walk the road you will find the way bordered by a mature, well layered hedge. Such hedges are as much a feature of this landscape as the ubiquitous ridge and furrow. For centuries, hedge and ditch have been the principal means by which the land has been divided. Long may they survive, and long may they escape the prairie approach to farming that has destroyed so much of the character of rural Britain.

Like a corrugated iron sheet: the fossilized landscape of ridge and furrow.

The road again crosses railway and canal, the railway this time in a cutting rather than perched up on an embankment. The canal here shows very clearly how the new 'modern' line was aimed at providing the shortest possible route. The visual impact of this new route remains, however, quite negligible, for you need to do no more than walk a few yards from the bridge for the whole canal to become all but invisible.

The next major feature on the landscape lies ahead, the village of Harborough Magna, stretching out along the ridge, the church tower forming a prominent landmark. It is a good example of a common type of village plan, with houses laid out on either side of the road. The extent of the village is very clearly defined and there is no difficulty in locating the old boundaries for, as you come into the village, the street name Back Lane appears. The back lane marks the edge of the settlement: on the village side tenement plots lead down to the houses; away from it the system of open fields takes over. So Harborough Magna has a simple and easily recognized form, though the village itself has been much altered over the years. There are some very interesting individual buildings, though many of the older houses have been maltreated by totally insensitive modernization. But look at little Acorn Cottage with its huge windows, a sure indication that the house was used for some form of work which required a great deal of light. In fact, the area round Coventry was busy in the nineteenth century with a thriving cottage industry, making ribbons. Cottages such as this usually held Jacquard looms which were used for weaving complex patterns. It was a notably unreliable trade, but ribbon weaving provided a useful addition to many a family income.

The little village shows great variety in its buildings, but none of the obvious signs of prosperity found near Newbold. Look at the church, for example, where only the front of the nave is graced with ashlar stone, and the rest of the building is of cruder, coursed rubble. Houses here often seem to lurk behind high walls, but when you reach the B4112 a new phase of development appears. The inn at the corner is basically an old building, and the steeply pitched roof and dormer windows indicate that it was once thatched. Now, however, the thatch has gone, replaced by corrugated iron, and new buildings spread out along the main road.

Follow the road down to Harborough Parva and then take the footpath that runs off to Cosford between the houses opposite the road junction (map reference 480789). This is a green lane, a

Snow fills the hollows and accentuates the patterns of ridge and furrow.

broad track between the fields where, yet again, ridge and furrow is conspicuous.

What exactly is ridge and furrow? Consider a team of oxen pulling a plough which turns over the sod rather than just scraping through the surface. The team goes up the field and then returns on a close, parallel track. The two sets of sods pile up to form a ridge. If the same field is ploughed over and over again for generations, following the same lines, then the ridges will grow higher and the furrows deeper. This is just what happened in the very constricted field systems that surrounded medieval villages. What we see here is a field system frozen at one particular moment in time. These are fields which were last ploughed and where crops last grew some five centuries ago. Sometimes hedges have been planted, cutting across the old fields as new enclosures have been made, but the old basic field pattern remains fixed.

What caused the sudden ending of the medieval ploughland? The answer is likely to appear in this part of the world in very tangible form; we can see it nibbling away at the grass-covered ridges – sheep. The late fifteenth century saw a great change from crop growing to sheep rearing. Britain was the world's greatest supplier of wool. Manufacturers at home and abroad were eager to buy high-quality fleeces, and there was more money for the landowner in sheep than was ever to be made from cereal crops. Grass was grown over the old open fields, and the implications of this change are enormous. It required many men to plough the fields, to tend and harvest the crops; a huge flock of sheep could roam over many fields and needed no more than one shepherd to care for it. And what effect did that have on the landscape? That will appear shortly, but first we have one more encounter with our transport story.

Walking across the fields towards Cosford is an increasingly noisy experience, thanks to the traffic on the M6, and the sight as well as the sound of the motorway soon begins to dominate the scene. Motorways have used up considerable quantities of land, and their visual impact has been immense. On the horizon you can see the bridge that takes the A426 across the motorway, a harsh line ruled against the sky, with no attempt being made to fit the bridge to its surroundings. It represents the brutalism of our time at its most extreme. Closer at hand, the way leads across a bridge

Humps and bumps in the fields are the remains of the village of Cosford, demolished so that sheep could graze.

over a disused railway, which was once in a cutting but is now being steadily filled in. Beyond that is the hamlet of Cosford.

The houses here have an air of prosperity and well-being. They are predominantly Georgian but have been much altered over the years – note the change in brick pattern showing where the first house has been extended upwards. It is a tiny settlement, yet the surrounding fields show that it must once have been very different. Look at the land to the west between the present houses and the stream. Here you can see a complex of ridges and bumps, which form themselves into regular patterns of squares and oblongs. The size and shape give an indication of their origin, for these bumps are all that remains of the former houses of the old village of Cosford. Throughout this part of the country you will find similar marks where villages have been entirely destroyed or, as here, dramatically reduced in size as the old arable land was given over to sheep. These humps and bumps tell a story of dispersed families and ruined communities. Here, on the ground, is one of the sadder tales from England's past.

From Cosford we now turn back across the fields to Newbold, the way marked by a tall chimney that stands like a beacon before us. On our way we see a repetition of the field pattern that has marked so much of our journey – the squared-off lines of well kept hedges as though drawn with a ruler over the older open fields. The track, heading south-west from the village, crosses the railway again. Here the infilling is almost complete, so that only the lines of trees that once bordered the tracks now mark the route. How strange that after no more than a century of use the traces of the railway are being obliterated! Soon perhaps only the brick bridge with its stone coping will give even a hint that trains ever came this way. It is one last example as we finish the walk back to Newbold-on-Avon of how our landscape is still perpetually changing.

WALK 6

SHIFTING SANDS

Route: *A circular walk from Walberswick Quay car park across Westwood Marshes to Newdelight Walks, Blythburgh and Walberswick (10 miles)*

Map: *OS Sheet 156 (1:50000 series)*

The first sound we heard in Walberswick was the cry of a curlew. For the rest of the walk, sounds and noises played a significant part in our understanding and appreciation of the landscape. Certainly all the senses help the landscape detective, but why were we so aware of sounds on this particular walk? Perhaps it was the constant reminder of Benjamin Britten operas on our journey by car to Walberswick, passing the famous concert hall converted from Snape Maltings, seeing signposts to Snape village, where Miss Baggott chased the sweeps, and on to Aldeburgh, the setting for *Peter Grimes*. It is perhaps not surprising that when we finally arrived at Walberswick by the estuary of the River Blyth (which means pleasant river) the bird cry brought to mind a later opera, *Curlew River*. The estuary itself offers a completely different environment from that of previous walks. Everywhere there are the sounds of the sea – water lapping under boats, the endless cry of the seagulls, ropes slapping aluminium masts and the hiss of shingle moved by the undertow.

The car park is in a flat space with the sea walls on one side leading up to the river bank. It is the sea we consider first. At Chollerford, the eastern abutment of the Roman bridge is isolated in a field several yards from the River Tyne, which had gradually changed its course over the years. Here the action of weather and tide is much greater and the distances involved are measured in miles rather than in yards. The first thing to notice is the sea defences. Concrete walls and earth banks surround the area. Sand dunes are covered in marram grass, a plant able to survive on the limited nutrition provided by the sand, but essential because its roots hold the dunes together and help prevent them being moved by wind and rain (it is often sown deliberately for this

Railway sleepers re-used to make a path through the reeds at Walberswick.

purpose). The whole of this coast is constantly being battered and changed, not only by the normal tides but by the harsher winter storms and floods. In fact, the combination of wind and tide has occasionally brought severe damage to these towns, causing hardship and tragedy and affecting the fortunes of the area.

The route follows the road away from the quay, past a pleasant house on the right which has stepped gables giving it a distinctly Dutch air. It is a reminder that this is the closest part of the coast to once hostile Holland. Several sea battles, notably the Battle of Sole Bay in 1672, were fought just off this shore. On the left is the old village green and an inn with an unusual cut-out inn sign. Adnams, the Southwold brewery, have an individual approach, a refreshing change from the national breweries' 'house colours'. The green is some distance from the quay and on high ground. Could the original quay have been here by the inn? At nearby Orford, the old quay can still be seen quite clearly a long way from the water. However, there is nothing to prove this hypothesis here. One feature normally found by the village green is missing – the church. One can assume that this is on still higher ground. Possibly the locals learned a lesson from nearby Dunwich, where several churches have disappeared beneath the sea.

Close to the green is an outhouse constructed of a building material not seen on previous walks – flint arranged roughly in rows or bands. Flint has been quarried in East Anglia for thousands of years. It is one of the purest forms of natural silica and as such is hard and very durable. Despite this, flint can be worked by hitting it sharply with a hammer – or in earlier times with a deer antler –

when it fractures or flakes. Thus it can be worked or knapped into shape. To the west of here near Weeting in Norfolk is Grimes Graves, where flints were mined four thousand years ago.

The main road continues to rise through the village, but our route is through a gap in the sea wall by an unusual thatched shelter. As you pass through, look at the gate. Although it is only about two foot in height it bridges the gap to the sea defence level, a continuous barrier stretching down the coast. Our path follows a route through a marshy area between the sea wall and firmer, higher ground. There is a maze of raised paths, bridges and streams with the main river flowing virtually parallel with and close to the sea, its banks strengthened with wooden pilings. In fact this, the Dunwich River, now misses the town of Dunwich altogether, after a change of course. Towards the sea, there are signs of Second World War defence systems, again a reminder of the proximity of Europe. As if to echo these thoughts the peace of the area was shattered during our walk by several jets flying in close formation near to the ground. The area's flat landscape is ideal for air force bases.

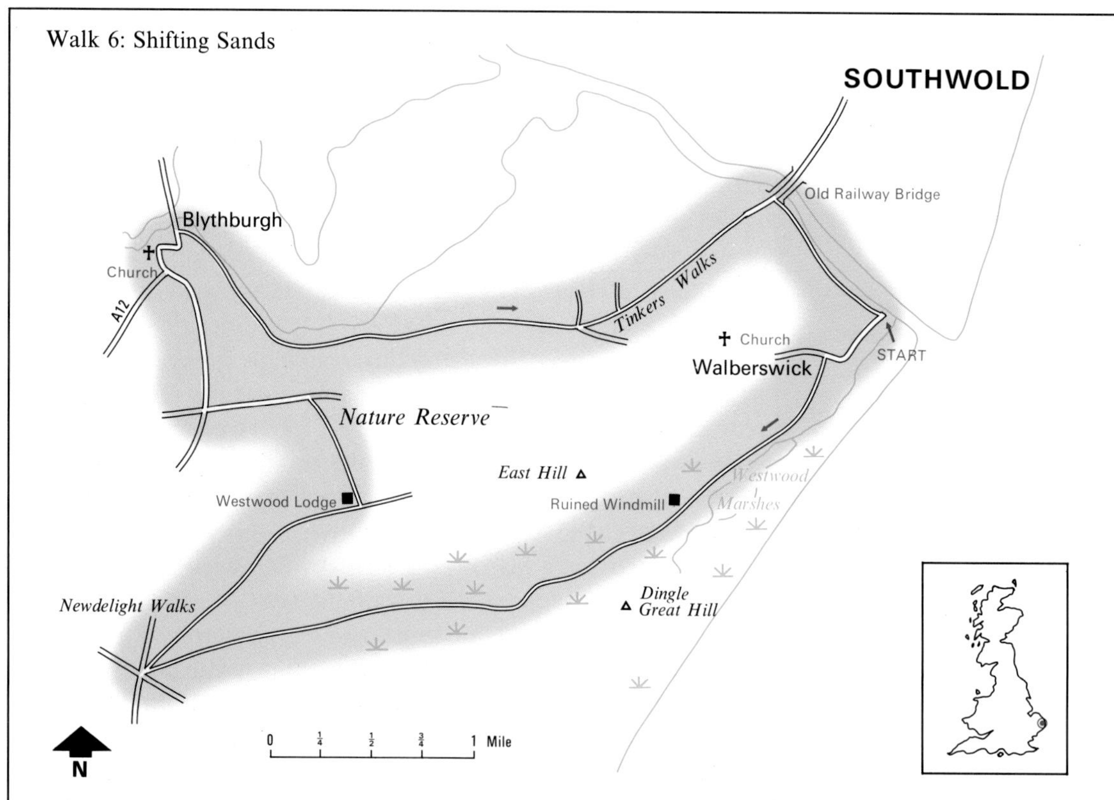

The cultivated reed beds give an indication of the windmill's use, isolated as it is in the marshes.

On both sides of the path, the reeds grow in quantity, not unlike fields of wheat rustling in the wind. The surface of the path changes from earth to railway sleepers – strange material to find in a marsh. They show little sign of wear and in general the marshland paths seemed well defined and well maintained. The path leads to a dyke crossed by a footbridge, but we continue along the north bank. Two landmarks now appear. Inland is the flint tower of Walberswick church, situated in the upper part of the village, protected from the sea by its height and from the wind by a belt of trees. The second landmark is our next objective, a round tower in the south. The river is now joined by winding streams as the water continually makes new channels. Alongside these streams grassy banks carry the path, which is occasionally blocked by an encroaching thicket. Forced to drop down to the reeds at one point, we found our feet sinking deep into the wet ground. The constant chatter of birdsong mingles with the sound of the shingle and, on the day we went, the dull, muted sound of a fog horn announced a thick sea mist, although we walked in sunshine. The round tower turns out to be the remains of a brick windmill, and there are still sections of its woodwork remaining, including what appears to be the tail pole. Its position close to the dyke wall, where there are signs of a culvert or sluice, indicates that it was a drainage mill, originally used to help adjust water levels in the marsh. There is a well preserved example of such a mill, which drives a scoop wheel, comparatively close by at Herringfleet. We later learned that there had been attempts to restore the mill in the 1950s but most of it was destroyed by fire in 1960. This area of marshland is managed rather like conventional farmland, except that the crop is reeds for thatching, not cereals. Tractor marks in the damp ground between the reeds confirm this.

The route leads past the mill and forks right at the signpost. Looking back, we saw men working on nets from a punt. The nets, suspended from floats, stretched some length down the river. The distance was too great for detail to be clear, but the nets may well have been set for eels. We tend nowadays to think of the punt as a pleasure craft, but they were originally designed for more serious use, the flat-bottomed vessel being ideal for navigating shallow streams and channels.

Further along the path the feeling of openness diminishes as high land begins to encroach, with Dingle Great Hill to the south and East Hill to the north. Reed beds still surround us but the vegetation along the path itself is now changing. Gorse is more frequent, occasionally necessitating a detour through the edge of the reed beds in order to avoid the prickles. As we approach the rising ground the vegetation changes again. Thickets and brambles increase and a tree stands by the path. Then there is a patch where the reeds grow more than head-high, giving an indication of what the uncultivated, unharvested marsh would have been like. It is somewhat reminiscent of Wicken Fen in Cambridgeshire, where the National Trust is preserving an area of original fenland.

The change in the vegetation is more pronounced as the ground becomes firmer and we enter a woodland of immature silver birch. The final character change from marsh to forest happens in yards. So too does the change in birdsong, as the shriek of seabirds gives way to the twitter of woodland species. The path is still discernible but is very sticky going, and often the walker has to make his way across branches laid over the bog. On the marshes there was an open feel but here the trees close in and it is dark and dank. Drainage channels full of brown, brackish water show the occasional bubble of marsh gas. There is no grass, only ferns, moss and a large amount of rotting vegetation, including quite large logs. This section of the walk is very wet and dirty and needs to be tackled with care. It has the look of a primeval forest.

At last the path becomes firmer and once again the vegetation changes quite suddenly to obviously managed woodland. There seems to be every shade of brown and green and the enclosed feeling of the wetland is lost as the path opens out to an area marked on the map as Newdelight Walks. Many such 'walks' are marked on the map. The *Oxford English Dictionary* gives various definitions of 'walk', all pertaining to tracts of land, usually for keeping animals, including sheep and gamecock. Perhaps the most appropriate definition here is 'a tract of land perambulated by a superintending officer', though East Sheep Walk, marked on the map at 480745, suggests another possible meaning (in the Middle Ages the wool trade made the port of Dunwich to the south one of the wealthiest in England). The map also marks a tumulus, so overgrown that without the map for identification it would be indistinguishable from any other lump on the ground.

The route turns east and almost back on itself as the path climbs steadily through heathland towards Westwood Lodge. On the left is a cottage with beehives in the garden. There is silver sand underfoot and on each side of the path are heathers and coverts of conifer. This is land for game birds. To the right is a view of the different bands of vegetation through which we have just walked. Quite large flints appear in the path, a reminder of the local building material. Surrounding the covert on the left is a clearly defined boundary bank like the one we saw in the Forest of Dean.

Westwood Lodge comes into sight. Built with a view over the sea, it stands imposing and isolated. The field opposite the house is full of hollows, possibly for quarrying, as former rubbish pits would be covered in nettles. Turning left past the barn, you get a less imposing but more interesting view of the house. It gives the impression of having been built in the seventeenth century, with drip mouldings over the windows. The barn by the house has the same stepped gables we saw at Walberswick. Follow the path to the B1387. There are wide views over the surrounding countryside as we are thrust into the landscape of modern farming. The fields stretch for a long way with old hedgerows and boundaries flattened. Here the past has been levelled.

At the road, you can see the River Blyth snaking to the sea from Blythburgh, whose church dwarfs the surrounding village. The route follows the road to the water-tower – a familiar landmark in this part of the country – and then turns right to the village. At the crossroads, Blacksmith's Forge Cottage illustrates a progression of building styles. One part is of flint construction with brick quoins and brick window surrounds; then come two extensions built in

Worked or knapped flint used as decoration in the wall of Blythburgh church.

different bricks. These may indicate later additions to the cottage, or a separation between living quarters and forge.

Blythburgh church is a complete surprise, simply because of its immense size. Local flint is used extensively and there are decorated panels of knapped flint contrasting with the whole stones. The walls are heavily buttressed, with two unusual flying buttresses at the east end, underneath which are doorways into the church. It is impossible to do justice to the interior in a few words, but some particularly impressive details deserve a mention. The floor is of plain brick. Attached to the tie beams of the roof are pairs of angels still showing bullet holes made by Cromwell's men in 1644. Over the south porch door is a replica of one of the angels, made by the Institute of Archaeology in 1977. To our eyes it may look vulgar but the original colours and materials have been faithfully reproduced, including – surprisingly – tinfoil. There are fine carved pew-ends representing the Seven Deadly Sins and a Tudor Jack the Lad, a painted figure that originally struck the hours on the clock. A narrow circular staircase leads to a meditation chapel, from which there is a good view of the carved figures decorating the nave. Inside the chapel the walls are plain flint, giving the room a rough, honest feel which echoes the text on the wall. 'Live more simply, that others may simply live.'

Why does such a small village have a church of such grandeur? When the church was built Blythburgh was a much more important place than it is today. It had two annual charter fairs, its own mint, a gaol and a market dating back to before the Norman Conquest. There was also a large quay, for here, despite fierce competition from Dunwich, many goods were loaded and

Changing features of the landscape: Blythburgh creek shows a variety of land forms and vegetation.

unloaded. But by the end of the fifteenth century Blythburgh had declined because larger ships could not navigate the river. Then in 1676 a fire damaged much of the town and drove many people away. Dunwich too was to decline and the records show a long battle with neighbouring Walberswick to attract trade. The sea was to have the last word, however, when a sandbank changed the direction of the river and isolated Dunwich. Walberswick survived, as we shall see later. The surviving buildings of Blythburgh to the west of the church are extremely beautiful and there is a lot of good detail to be seen. Look for the house with Tudor chimneys and casement windows, and a pink, symmetrical seventeenth-century house with a fine wrought-iron gate. On the far side of the river bundles of reeds are stacked awaiting transport.

The route continues past the White Hart to a footpath signposted to Walberswick through a National Nature Reserve. Much is being done in this area to preserve the wild life. The high ground by Westwood Lodge is now behind us and we are back at sea level. Across the river is an avenue of trees – probably the sign of an early crossing-point by ford or ferry – but looking back to the village there is no trace of the old large town or its harbour. However, for the first time on the walk we see farm animals, a few sheep and cows in the meadow, a reminder of the old system that existed before the change to arable and the destruction of the hedgerow. We are again back with the reeds of the marshes and the overwhelming curtain of birdsong. Out on the mudflats the waders shovel the mud with their flat bills. The river winds through in its meandering course. Our path begins to climb to firm ground, with woodland developing. Under the lee of the hill the trees show healthy growth and it is interesting to note how woods develop when left on their own. For example, one can see

A bridge too high at Walberswick: the present pedestrian bridge has been lifted above the level of the original swing bridge that carried the light railway.

how little grows beneath the widespread branches of the oak. Where the path reaches the road two humps covered in ferns betray the presence of another set of tumuli.

Follow the road towards Walberswick and after a few hundred yards a straight embankment appears, running parallel with the road and on its left. It is not unlike the covert boundary we saw earlier, except that it is extremely level. Our route now turns left by the farm onto a footpath signposted Walberswick. Looking back, there is very little to indicate the origin of the embankment, but its line, differentiated by bushes, continues to the north-east. Gorse grows in profusion, suggesting a different soil from that of the surrounding land. It now seems unlikely that we are looking at a boundary. Then, where footpaths cross, all becomes clear. The remains of a bridge are followed by a considerable cutting. We have reached the line of the old Southwold Light Railway. All the accounts of the railway deem it one of great character, known to a former resident as 'Poppity'. Later the cutting broadens out. Is this the nearest point to Walberswick and as such the town's halt? There are no signs to help us, not even a sleeper. These have all been taken away to be used elsewhere (we met some of them on our path across the marshes). The line continues as a footpath to a bridge across the river, though it seems too high to be the railway bridge. Investigation shows it to be a modern bailey bridge. This replaced an earlier swing bridge and the extra height was necessary to allow boat traffic to pass underneath. At the bridge there is a typical estuary vista. On the left are the remains of a tower mill, very like the one we saw earlier. Over the bridge the line of the railway can be clearly seen heading for Southwold with its prominent water-tower and lighthouse. Our route follows the south bank of the river towards the sea.

The sounds have changed again to the noises of the creek, of water draining into the river from the marshes through a simple one-way valve operated by the pressure of water on a weighted flap (a device we shall meet again in Somerset). There are many signs that this is a working river. Among the pleasure yachts are fishing boats, the letters on their sides revealing their registration ports.There are fishing huts on the bank, some selling fish, and a lifeboat station. The huts are in good repair and cared for, being in regular use, unlike the tatty beach huts visited once a year by absentee landlords. Down at the quay are houses built on stilts as protection against high tides. They stand close to a slope with a rusted winch, the last traces of a ferry. And so the circle is complete.

The 'fish for sale' sign demonstrates that Walberswick creek is not just a place for pleasure boats.

Simple jetties, constructed with available timbers, line the creek at Walberswick.

WALK 7 RHYNES, CLYSES AND HUNKY PUNKS

Route: *Westonzoyland, Middlezoy, Othery, Burrow Bridge, Moorland, Westonzoyland (9 miles)*

Map: *OS Sheet 182 (1:50 000 series)*

Rhynes, clyses and hunky punks, words unfamiliar and strange to most of us, are common enough in this area – which itself can seem equally strange. This is a walk through the Somerset Levels. At first glance the area might seem to have much in common with the wetlands of East Anglia that we have just left, but there is a crucial difference, for the levels cover a huge area of some 250 square miles, spreading far inland. On the map, the obvious features are the sea which forms one boundary and the hills which complete the enclosure. Water drains down from the hills into rivers that often prove inadequate to hold the floods, and this gives the area its character and its problems – problems exacerbated by a narrow ridge of clay between the levels and the sea. The water draining down into this great natural sink is not easily removed, and high tides climbing up the river valleys can cause still more difficulties. Yet even a quick glance at the map shows that the levels are not uniformly flat. Humps and bumps appear and have become the focal points of settlement, the most famous being Glastonbury Tor. Our walk does not take us there, but the influence of Glastonbury Abbey was once felt throughout the region.

The walk starts at one of these island settlements, or 'sowys' as they were known – a name that changed over the years to 'zoys'. Westonzoyland stands on one of the most prominent lumps on this flat land, and makes itself even more prominent by a magnificent church tower rising to a height of just over a hundred feet. The church dominates not just the village but all the surrounding countryside, a building of great beauty and dignity which makes an ideal starting-point for the walk – not least because there is so little difficulty in finding it. The earliest identifiable feature in the building is a tiny lancet window of about 1200, but most of what we see dates from the fourteenth and fifteenth centuries. One clear piece of dating evidence tells us of the dependence of the church on the abbey at Glastonbury. On the main buttress on the south transept are carved the initials R.B. – for Richard Beere, abbot from 1493 to 1525. But, fine as the outside is, the church's greatest glory lies inside. Open the door, walk through and stop to wonder at the magnificent roof, where angels spread their wings from the king-posts. Let your eye move down over the window tracery, typical of Somerset and here seen at its very best. It appears to be the model of a peaceful country church, but now turn back and look at the door through which you entered. It is heavily studded and bears a massive lock. It seems more in keeping with a prison than a church and, indeed, the church did serve briefly as a gaol. In 1685, the Duke of Monmouth's rebellion ended at the Battle of Sedgemoor, fought just outside the village. Five hundred rebels were held in the church, of whom five died of their wounds and twenty-two were later hanged.

Outside the church, it soon becomes clear how the special nature of this landscape has affected the development of the village. Buildings are confined to the high ground, so that village houses, inns and farms sit cheek by jowl. There are some fine buildings here, of which the purely functional buildings are by no means the least appealing. Opposite the church, for example, is an excellent stone barn with a contrasting hipped roof of bright red pantiles. The rather plain nineteenth-century house opposite the church is enlivened by some pointed arched windows said to have come from a monastic building. And you can find reminders of the social history of Westonzoyland, such as the Church of England Sunday and Weekly Schoolroom of 1840. As you walk down the main road to the east, there seems to be little to distinguish it from any other road, but the map shows that it follows a very slight ridge, which keeps it above flood levels. There are indications that this has been an important road for some time. A large inn fronts the road and a milestone can be seen on the right hand side as you walk away from the church. Most such milestones are survivors from the turnpike age, when the turnpike trusts were forced by Parliament to erect them, together with signposts, as a condition of being allowed to build the roads and collect tolls for their use.

At the end of the village, opposite the minor road to Liney, turn right onto the wide track that leads towards Middlezoy. At first sight the wide expanse of field to the east might suggest that the area had succumbed to the modern trend towards prairie farming – the creation of huge fields by the wholesale destruction of ancient hedgerows – but the numerous small brick and concrete buildings are easily recognizable as Second World War structures, and the area is quickly identified as a former airfield. One sometimes forgets just how many airfields were constructed during the war years and what a pronounced effect they have had on local landscapes. The land to the west shows quite different characteristics. The gently rising land around the village is used for crops ranging from cereals to vegetables, but set in small, enclosed fields. Given how little high ground there is to be shared out among the villagers, the small divisions are not surprising, nor is it surprising still to find a low degree of mechanization here. But these fields are no more than a brief prelude to the main theme of the walk; lines of willows marching across the horizon herald the arrival of the wetlands of the moor. The land is a chequerboard of fields of lush meadow grass with a large number of plants, such as the lovely yellow iris, that tell you at once that you are entering a watery environment. In this landscape, divisions between fields are rarely made in a conventional way by hedge or fence, but by ditches known locally as rhynes. They serve an obvious purpose as drains but they also act as moats, keeping the cattle which graze on the meadows within their fields – though the authors did feel rather nervous at finding nothing more than a narrow strip of water between themselves and a very large bull. Out on the moor the land does provide good grazing, though this is not the only use to which it is put. The willows that line the rhynes also have an important part to play in the local economy, which we shall explore later.

At the approach to Middlezoy the land begins to rise again and, though the 'island' only climbs to 20 metres above sea level, the whole nature of the country changes. The track which across the open moor had been delineated by rhynes now transforms itself into a typical West Country lane, sunk down between high banks topped by hedgerows. The long grass of the water meadows gives way to the short, coarser grass of the dry island. An apple orchard stands beside the path which climbs up towards the church. Again, as at Westonzoyland, the church makes a very prominent landmark and in outward appearance is very reminiscent of its larger neighbour. It was here we first met the phrase 'hunky punks' – a splendid name for the gargoyles, the strange grimacing beasts that

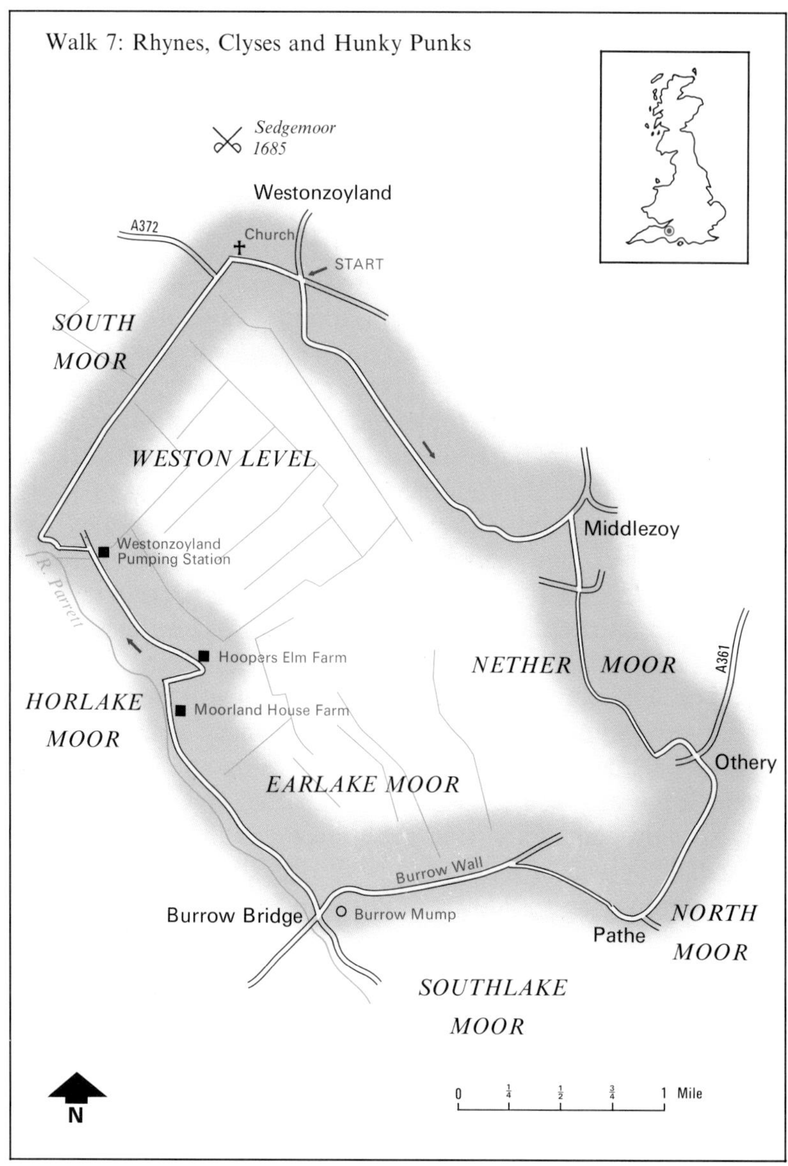

peer down from the tower. Inside, however, the church is comparatively simple, with a plain barrel vaulted roof.

This church too was dependent on the abbey of Glastonbury. The view from the churchyard is particularly fine – a wide panorama of the levels stretching out to the hills and at least one prominent, isolated knoll which we shall be seeing later. The pattern of regular square enclosures suggests that this is a comparatively modern field system designed to a plan rather than one developed over the centuries. The very regularity also indicates that it has not been adapted from an earlier system. This is our first clue towards putting a date to the drainage of this section of the old marsh.

Opposite the church is a curious building which seems to have strayed into Somerset from East Anglia, for it appears at first sight to be constructed of knapped flint. But this is not flint country. There are, however, extensive beds of a very similar material, chert, near the Somerset–Devon border. Like flint, chert can be knapped, and, as here, stones of different colours can be used to produce decorative effects. The house soon proves to be the odd man out. As you walk down the main street, Somerset vernacular architecture becomes the order of the day: thatched cottages, colour-washed walls and farms with yards opening straight on to the street. The thatch is all in excellent condition and often highly decorative (look for the thatch peacock on one roof). In many ways, such cottages are in a better state now than at any time in their history, for the motor car has meant that families no longer have to live next to their place of work. The picturesque farm cottage has become the desirable residence. There is, however, one reminder that even quite recently the village was a self-sufficient place. The village post office was also the store, the place to make phone calls and the local petrol station. Our path now turns off past the post office and leads across the fields to Othery.

Drainage ditches, or rhynes, criss-cross the Middle Levels, with attendant wetland vegetation.

At Othery, the church is again the dominant feature although it has come down the size scale by another division from Middlezoy. It has some interesting details. There is a fine George and Dragon above the door, but look in particular at the outside, where a buttress has been pierced to allow light to the window behind, a splendid example of how a later addition to a building was adapted to accommodate an earlier detail. Cross over the main road outside the church and take the minor road round to Pathe. On your left you will see a tall chimney, which might suggest the use of steam power. The first inclination is to assume that it must have something to do with land drainage, but it is set too far from any drain or rhyne for that to be the answer. As the only obvious land use in the area is agricultural, the next guess would be that this is part of an old steam-powered grain mill, and later checking proves that to be the correct answer.

A straggle of houses and cottages follows the road from Othery, many of them with large kitchen gardens making the most of this

Burrow Mump: the one hill in the Middle Levels, which served as a lookout point.

A house by the Parrett which provides numerous clues to former use. The section to the left without windows on the upper storey is quite different from the domestic section to the right. The large squat chimney and the sluice suggest that a steam engine was once housed here for land drainage.

narrow ridge of land. The name 'Mill Farm' alerts you to look for a mill building beside the stream that follows the road. A building duly appears, its gable end parallel to the stream and showing signs in the shape of large bricked-in openings of having been adapted to domestic use from an earlier way of life. Signs of water power being used are not apparent, however, so, as sometimes happens in these cases, one is left with likelihoods rather than certainties.

The road now turns through 180° and at the apex of the bend a wide track leads out across the fields. Such tracks are known locally as 'droves' and do indeed provide access to the grazing fields from the roadway. Up ahead is Burrow Mump, the prominent mound we saw from Middlezoy, topped by a ruined chapel. This is our next landmark, but first take the drove that runs north towards the main road, the A361. As you reach it you find first a ditch then a substantial bank, both of which follow the line of the road – or, to be more accurate, the road follows the line of the bank. This is a truly massive earthwork which looks to be exactly what it is, a very old divider of the land. It is in fact the medieval Burrow Wall, built to divide Southlake Moor from Earlake Moor. It had a double function, acting as a causeway joining Othery to Burrow Bridge and as a barrier to flood water. It was built in the middle of the thirteenth century and like much of the early reclamation work of the marshes was paid for by Glastonbury Abbey. It represents one of the earliest steps in the long battle to reclaim the land of the Somerset Levels.

You can now continue on down the main road, which tends to

Flat fields neatly divided into squares show the pattern of land drainage and enclosure.

be busy and noisy, or retrace your steps to the main drove, but in either case head towards Burrow Mump. This is a natural feature and one of some importance in the history of the region. Alfred the Great took refuge at Athelney in what was then the middle of the marshes, and here he rallied his forces for the fight against the Danes. The mump is an obvious strategic lookout for guarding the approaches to Alfred's island shelter. Climb to the top and you have a commanding view of all the surrounding country. Subsequently a Norman castle was built here, followed by a church, and a second church, begun in the eighteenth century but never completed. It is the latter building which crowns the hill today.

The way now continues along the eastern bank of the river Parrett. Man has clearly had a great deal to do with the present course of the river. The banks are built up extremely high, though to understand why this is necessary you have to travel right down to the estuary. On most of the rivers that cross the moor the mouth is protected from flooding at high tides by clyses. These are simply heavy flaps set in a dam which allow water to flow unhindered down river to the sea but are closed off by high tides. The mouth of the Parrett is too wide for such structures, so tides can still sweep far inland. The banks do, however, provide good firm land for building on and houses follow the roadways along the bank tops.

These buildings are almost all of the eighteenth and nineteenth centuries – further evidence that this was a period of major reclamation work. Look out for one especially interesting building on the opposite bank next to the small clyse which controls the flow of a subsidiary stream or sluice. The house next to it is quite large, but the end nearest the sluice does not have windows on its two floors to fit the pattern of the rest of the building. This suggests that one end was not a dwelling at all, and its position by the drain also suggests some sort of pumping station with a cottage attached. It was, in fact, a steam engine-house and cottage, but there are no longer any other outward signs.

Westonzoyland Pumping Station. The water is pumped off the land and through sluices into the River Parrett.

The preserved Westonzoyland pumping engine. A similar engine was once housed in the house shown on the previous page.

Introduction of powerful steam pumps must have made a huge difference to the drainage of the area and hence to the value of the land. That prosperity is reflected in the size and grandeur of the buildings, houses and farms. Moorland House, for example, is a very elegant piece of Georgian architecture, with parkland planted with trees in the best style of the period. But this was also the period of window taxes and in order to save both money and the essential symmetry of the house fake windows were painted on the façade.

Now the road turns right towards Hoopers Elm Farm, again with parkland round it. But note the factory-type bell over the farmyard, bringing Victorian notions of urban order and regularity to the countryside. Half a mile further on a track leads down beside a rhyne to a building with a prominent tall chimney stack. This is Westonzoyland pumping station.

By the beginning of the nineteenth century all that could be done in the way of land reclamation by cutting new drainage channels had been done, but over in East Anglia experiments with steam-powered pumps were proving successful. It was decided to try the idea on the levels and the first steam pump in the region was installed on this site in 1830. This was of the type you can still see on the Fens at Stretton, a beam pump and scoop wheel. In time it was decided that a new engine was needed, which was duly installed in 1861. In 1951 the small diesel pumping station which now stands over the drain was set to work. But, thanks to the work of volunteers, the old steam engine survives. The pumping station is regularly open to visitors and the engine is occasionally steamed again. Steam enthusiasts will no doubt be interested to hear that this is a unique Easton and Amis 2-cylinder engine which drove a centrifugal pump. Enthusiasts and non-enthusiasts alike should be impressed by the fact that this comparatively small engine kept 2,000 acres of land clear of water, draining roughly the area contained within our walk. Altogether there were eight such stations on the river. There are many interesting features to see at this site, not least the pumping engine itself. It is surprising to find that the flywheel is set with wooden and not metal teeth, but there is a sound practical reason for this: if anything went wrong the teeth were the first things to break, not the more expensive machine parts. A small blacksmith's forge on the site took care of maintenance. The trust which runs the engine also displays other

This high bank dates back to medieval times, when it was built as a flood barrier. That it is old can be deduced from the houses built on top of it.

exhibits, though not all are directly connected with the running of the pumps.

Now begin the return to Westonzoyland along the minor road. Again there is a very prominent bank at the road side, and again it must be old for old houses are built on top of it. This is another medieval work similar to the Burrow bank, this time separating South Moor from the Weston Level. The land on either side is crossed by numerous ditches with their ubiquitous accompaniment of pollarded willows.

The willows are an important resource. They are regularly cut back to allow new shoots, or withies, to form. These are harvested when they are about six feet long; some withies are also grown as a field crop. Along the road on the right-hand side you can see bundles of withies stacked against a simple hut, beside which is a low brick structure with a chimney at one end. This is where the withies are stripped of their bark. The brick structure is in fact a boiler, in which the wood is heated for eight hours to soften the bark. This is then stripped off by machine. The stripped withies are dried, tied into bundles and are ready for taking to market, where they are sold for basket making. It is a local craft which, in its essentials, has changed little over the centuries.

Looming up ahead, the church tower of Westonzoyland announces the completion of our circuit.

A local industry: bundles of withies which will eventually be used for basket making.

WALK 8

UP HILL AND DOWN DALE

Route: *Skipton Castle, Embsay, Rylestone Fell, Skipton (11 miles)*

Map: *OS Sheets 103 and 104 (1:50 000 series)*

The most imposing feature in the centre of Skipton is the castle, and this is where our walk starts. Earlier settlements undoubtedly existed, but the clues in this walk show how Skipton's development has unfolded from the castle, with its medieval settlement, to the present day. Just as the people of Skipton from the thirteenth century onwards were dependent on the castle for their safety, so the town itself was dependent on the surrounding hills for its existence.

The heart of the castle is the old part around Conduit Court. The great hall is protected on one side by high cliffs and on the other by a series of joined circular towers. These were built so that missiles were deflected and an attacker could be seen and fired at from any point along the walls. The conduit itself was once the castle's water supply in time of siege. So successful was the castle's design that in 1642 it withstood a siege for three years. There is a lot to see but two things are worth singling out. First the garderobes, functional but primitive lavatories, projecting over the castle walls with holes above the moat. Second, in the gatehouse one room is completely covered in coral shells – a very popular eighteenth-century decoration.

From the gatehouse, the newer parts of the castle come into view. They echo the older shape, but slits are replaced by grand windows – progress in armaments made early defensive design obsolete and squabbles were increasingly settled in courts, not in the field of battle. Outside and to the left of the castle is Bailey Road, named for the large outer wall of the castle. The route follows the footpath by the wall. There is a set of limestone steps and in a field across the road we see sheep, our first sight of the reason for Skipton's development.

The path signposted to Embsay follows the wall, which is built with mortar at the start, and then as drystone walling, with a pronounced batter, or slope. Looking back towards the rear of the castle we see two small stone bridges exactly in line. The ground between them is smooth and on a slope, which suggests an entrance to a lower part of the castle, though no further clue can be seen. On either side of the road to Embsay we see the now familiar lumps and bumps caused by quarrying, and the hill to the right has extensive signs of man-made shaping. Lower down, a railway line circles the hill to join the road close to Embsay station. It crosses the road on a good double bridge and it is clear that, although they are adjacent, the two arches of the railway bridge serve different purposes. The first provides access for farm livestock, which can thus pass safely under the railway without using the road, which is crossed by the second arch. It seems an expensive way to keep a few sheep from the highway but shows the lengths transport engineers had to go to in order to accommodate land users. As a contrast to this rather large bridge the first of many little stone bridges is visible, made necessary by the uneven land and the many small streams. The line divides just before Embsay station, where it is being restored for steam running as far as Bolton Abbey by the Yorkshire Dales Railway Museum Trust.

After an unimposing start the village takes on more character. Next to the Cavendish Arms is a barn with a dovecot, and opposite is the sign to a Courtaulds mill. The pavement is raised and starts with steps. On the left split-level houses show how the builder has adapted to the terrain and built into the hillside. The mill itself is up West Lane opposite the station, and it appears still to be working, for bundles of cloth are lying around outside. What appeared from the road to be a small mill turns out to be a large complex with all the classic signs of industrial work. The main mill, invisible from the front, is a weaving mill, probably originally powered by steam, as there is a chimney close by. The mill's roof is of a dog-tooth design, with the vertical sides glazed. These windows, like all weaving shed windows, face north. The north gives the purest and most even light – essential in the weaving industry so that the finished cloth is consistent in texture and colour (and also sought after by artists for the same reasons).

The path leads to the older part of the village. As we approach the high ground we are back among farm buildings and agricultural life, which is borne out by the name of the road where the route turns to the left, Pasture Road. Along this road is a very traditional stone house dated 1665, with many fine features. On the other side of the road a stream has been diverted, controlled and dammed in order to make a header pond for the mill. The pond is long and narrow, following the contours of the hillside. There is a humped bridge and beside it a sign for a tannery, which indicates the presence of an industry usually detected by smell. Further along on the right the diversions to the natural stream are seen. The stream is carefully channelled with aqueducts and sluices and its bed is lined with squared stones, or sets, to prevent erosion.

Continue uphill to Hill Top Farm – a good example of a traditional farm, still in use and in good condition. We found that where crofts and farms were still in use all the year round the drystone walls were in a good state of preservation, but when these buildings had a non-agricultural or occasional use the walls were in a poor state of repair – an exact analogy with the fishermen's huts on the Walberswick walk. At this crossing of the paths the walker may choose to take a short cut by following the path signposted to None-Go-Bye Farm and rejoining the walk there; the main route heads north uphill towards Embsay reservoir. On the right you get glimpses of an industrial chimney, and as this comes into full view you can see that the land surrounding it displays unmistakable signs of quarrying. It is not possible to get close to the chimney as it is on private land. Its isolated position is the result of the local presence of lead ore, which was dug out of the hills and smelted *in situ*.

The farm on the left is called Intake Farm, which gives a clue to the sheep-farming methods of the area, intake and out-take farming. Up on the tops past the reservoir – amongst the odd shepherd's hut, shelter pens and walling, all built in stone quarried close by – is the out-take area. Here, in the milder months of the year, the sheep roam the tops feeding as best they can and are provided with occasional shelter. Then in the harsher months they move to the intake; they are brought down to the farms for more substantial shelter, winter grazing, lambing and slaughter.

At Embsay reservoir there is a folly-like building housing the works together with circular stone overflows. It seems that water boards retain the ability to build structures which are both functional and aesthetically unusual, if not appealing. You only have to think of Kew engine-house or the domed pumping station at Perth. Again the Walberswick walk is brought to mind by the sound of dinghy rigging knocking against aluminium masts in the wind, a sound unusual at an altitude of 700 feet above sea level.

From here the route rises over the tops to Norton Tower then

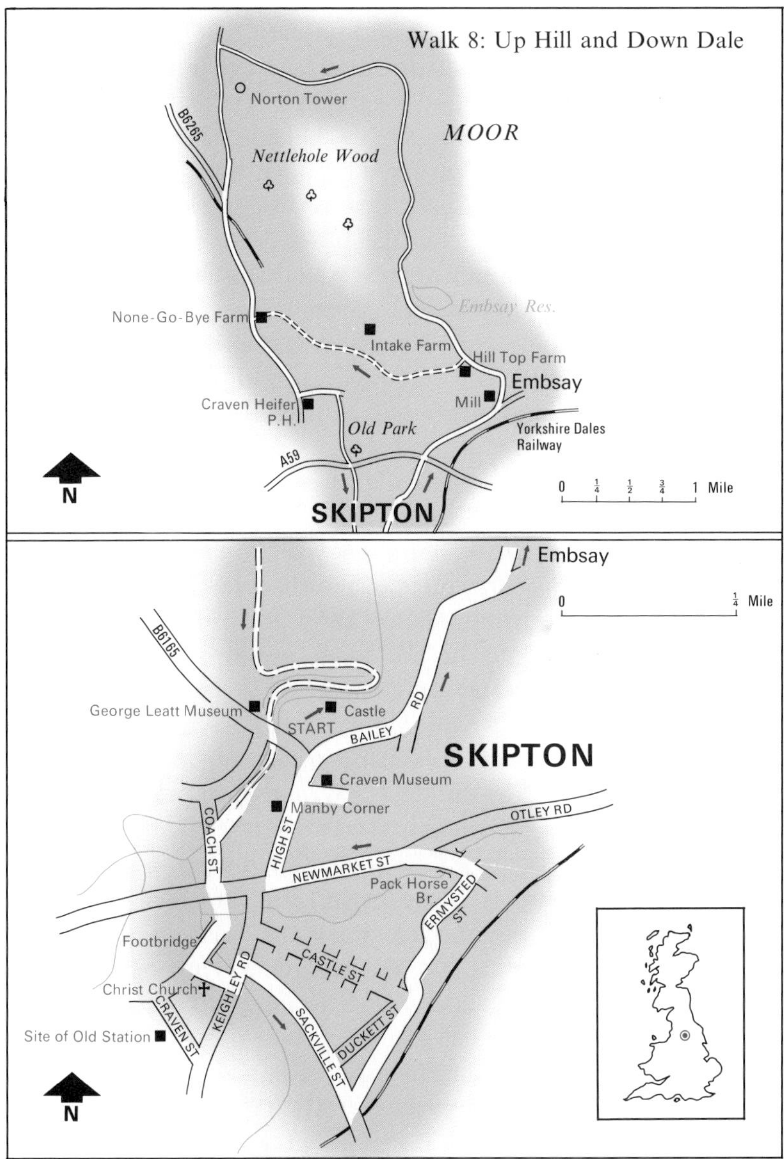

south along the footpath to join the B6265 at SD 974558. There are no specific landmarks on this route and the landscape detective should find his own way. Keep to well-worn paths, avoid fenced-off plantations and cross drystone walls only where there is a stile – they can be easily damaged by people climbing on them. Dogs should be left behind: this is sheep country.

The first thing to do on reaching the top of the rise is to look back towards Skipton. The town sits below the moors at a point where a pass joins Airedale to neighbouring Wharfedale, a good place for a market and for an industrial centre that utilizes the

At Embsay, the millpond is terraced into the hill and is overlooked by a fine seventeenth-century stone house.

area's resources. Embsay Crag, which also gives superb views over the valley, is itself a fine example of how the hill has weathered to reveal the bare rock and the geological strata. Looking down from here on to Nettlehole Wood we see signs of forest management – areas of different trees, new plantations and fellings. Drystone

Stone walls enclose small areas for intake farming as compared with the large expanse of moorland for out-take.

A drystone wall on the Skipton moors which must have taken some effort to construct.

walls are everywhere. Those on steep ground are especially impressive, with very large stone blocks which must have been very difficult to set in place. In summer, sheep dominate the landscape, well scattered because in the out-take they have to forage over a large area. Under foot there is a variety of surfaces, rock alternating with soggy peat, and the wide green track between the walls giving way to narrow paths through the heather. Norton Tower appears, built as the name suggests by the Nortons and immortalized in *The White Doe of Rylestone* by Wordsworth, who described it as 'an edifice of warlike frame'. It is interesting to match this description with the present structure and also to note how Wordsworth's description of the surrounding landscape coincides with our own experience. There is a multitude of sounds – sheep bleating, wind in the trees, a burst of birdsong and the unique sound of water cascading down a hillside.

Where the footpath rejoins the road it crosses the freight line from Grassington, which joins the main line at Skipton. Further down the road is None-Go-Bye Farm, where the footpath from Hill Top Farm rejoins the main walk. At the Craven Heifer pub – named, as the sign states, after a cow born in 1807, which weighed 176 stone 4 lb at the age of four years and was bred by the Reverend William Carr of Bolton Abbey – the route turns along Short Lee Lane (grid reference 982536) and then south down a public footpath by a cast-iron sign marked Skipton. This is a very rural path with hedgerows replacing stone walls and meadow replacing uneven tufts of heather. Despite the appearance of lowland pasture, arable farming would be impossible here: the soil is too full of stone. From the top of the hill, Skipton is laid out before us.

Most of Skipton was built during the Industrial Revolution, grafted on to a medieval market town. The medieval town is very obvious. A wide street running from the castle accommodates the market, while the surrounding area is a hotchpotch of narrow streets at all angles. This was the town as market centre, when a family lived and traded on its own home ground, each shopkeeper wanting as much shop frontage as close to the axis of the market as possible. Thus building after building was crammed into every available space. Around this nucleus grew the areas of the Industrial Revolution. A complex system of textile mills is set near to their two essentials: a supply of water, and an established trade route. Families no longer both worked and lived at home; they worked in the mill and lived in regimented terraces of stone houses.

A white concrete lump of an office block protrudes from the centre of the town. The mills were surrounded by mill houses, but there are no equivalent office houses round the office block. Increased mobility brought by the motor car means that employees no longer have to live next to their work. Similarly, trading estates and a housing estate have been added on to the outside of the industrial area. (It is instructive to compare the architect-designed estate and the materials used in its construction with earlier developments.)

The path now crosses the bypass, a sign of greater mobility, and we reach a small wood on the left. This is all that remains of Skipton Forest, large enough in 1302 to be supplying substantial quantities of wood, nuts, turf, honey and wax, according to contemporary receipts. A stile in the left-hand corner of the field takes the route to the top of Chapel Hill, where we turn left and cross the Eller Beck by a white footbridge. To the left of the bridge is a track that rises in a smooth incline and is bordered by a boundary wall. We are now at the rear of the castle. It is an extension of the path with the bridges that we saw at the beginning of the walk. Follow the path beside the beck to the east, and you come upon a magnificent view of the castle, which presents the same daunting prospect as that faced by would-be attackers in earlier times.

The water here is still and on a higher level than the Eller Beck. Opposite is a wharf with a dismantled stone building and set into its banks are several iron chutes. The still water must be that of a canal, man-made by blasting a channel out of solid rock. In fact this is the Springs Branch of the Leeds and Liverpool Canal, whose main line is about 700 yards away. Stone was brought here for loading on to boats from the quarries at Haw Park. Now there are three levels of water connected by overflows, the top level controlled by sluices. To all this the castle presents an incredible backdrop with its heavy buttresses and a good view of the garderobes from the outside.

Our path turns out to be the towpath and on the right a mill comes into view with a loading gantry over the canal. This is High Corn Mills, originally part of the Skipton Estate and now the George Leatt Industrial and Folk Museum. It is open to the public, and visitors can see the details of the milling process. Grain is released slowly into the centre of a slowly rotating millstone. It is ground to flour and carried outwards by the dressing of the stones to be collected round the outside. There are two very practical details to note. The first is the bell which alerts the miller if grain is not entering the stones. If the stones touched, the carefully dressed surfaces would be quickly damaged. The second is the mechanism which shakes the grain evenly on to the bedstone. Because of its constant clacking noise, it was known as the maiden's tongue. Various pieces of belt-driven machinery are powered by two overshot water-wheels. Like so many private museums, it offers a clutter of bits and pieces collected with a fondness for objects rather than to meet an educational aim, and the visit is reminiscent of poking round a good junk shop. One particular bonus was to find that stand-by power was provided by a 1916 Crossley gas engine (we meet another in Abingdon). There was also the statutory mill cat.

Farther along the towpath we reach an area where stone is used in many different ways. Large rough-hewn chunks serve as coping

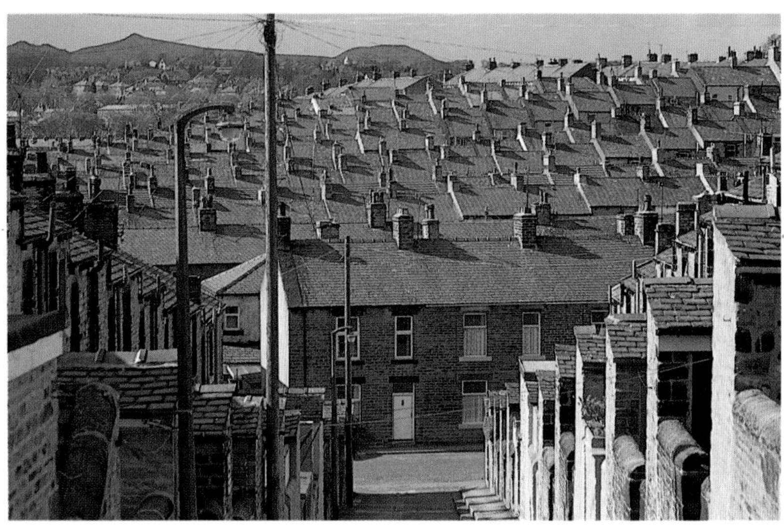

The regimented terraces of mill workers' houses in Skipton.

This footbridge at Skipton shows economic design and use of materials.

stones for walls; dressed stones, tightly bonded, give an imposing air to municipal buildings; and irregularly shaped pieces are used in drystone walling. Sadly, one piece of drystone walling has been repaired with cement. Was this a reflection of cost, design or 'craftsmanship'? There is also a wooden footbridge of extremely economic design, a single, narrow plank of wood with sides broadening into a V shape. Here the tail-race of the mill meets the beck, which falls away from the canal level. Cross the bridge over the canal by the Royal Shepherd pub and continue down Coach Street. Here the commercial canal complex is obvious. What was the wharf warehouse is now the Dales Outdoor Centre, but the cobbled yard, cranes and gateposts provide clues to how the wharf was run in earlier years.

The canal is crossed by a footbridge at the end of Water Hill. All around are signs of industrial activity. However, when Christ Church is reached there is a fine residential terrace in the middle of which sits the Railway Inn. The railway station is found to be some distance away along Black Walk. Later research showed this to be a second station, built in 1876 to replace an earlier one sited next to Craven Street and thus near the inn.

Straight across from Keighley road bridge is the Roasting Pot, which sells Yorkshire pies – as individual to the area as oatcakes

A local foundry made this cast-iron cover for a rubbish chute.

are to the Potteries. Later, in the Royal Shepherd, we feasted on this delicacy, served in the traditional way – that is, covered in mushy peas accompanied by mint sauce and eaten with a spoon from a bowl.

Further along Sackville Street is a yard with a sign advertising the two traditionally linked trades of joiner and undertaker. Past this, rows of terraced houses climb the hill. Many of the terraces have a traditional corner shop. As you go past Duckett Street to Upper Sackville Street one of the town mills can be seen across the canal. At the corner of the site there is an engine-house with the accompanying boiler house and chimney and weaving sheds with northern lights. At the top of the road is the freight line we have seen before. Following the little track along the top of the cutting you can see how the railway curves around the town in order to gain height for the climb to Grassington. Look at the details of the engineering works, bridges and cuttings, complete with lines of stone scree on the cutting banks which act as drainage channels.

The next feature of the walk is at the north end of Ermystead Street. On the way there it is worth looking at various details in the terraced streets. First, from high up there is a superb panorama of roofs showing the patterns of alleys. Second, look at the details of house decoration, porches, shared glass canopies, rough stone used as decoration in gardens, cast-iron rubbish flaps, stone door surrounds. At one point we had a glimpse through a window of a wooden staircase, obviously made by a craftsman. One wonders how many of these features were designed to a master plan.

In front of the old grammar school is the packhorse bridge, a reminder of the time when wool and cloth were carried on horseback. It is now unused and superseded, its path replaced by wider streets. But the inn next to it still has recognizable stables; and Newmarket Street still has old sets in its surface and a mill stream at its side.

And so to the changing face of the High Street. The market is still there, but a department store has absorbed the theatre and an inn, and most of the little alleys, or ginnels, have disappeared. Municipal buildings, erected as the town grew, have been turned into shops as political power became centralized; multiple stores with modern fascias have replaced older local establishments. One notable exception is the shop at Manby corner, which has a splendid front proclaiming itself as an ironmonger and iron foundry. The foundry itself is down a ginnel opposite the shop. Its cast-iron windows were, one hopes, made on the site.

Completing the circle of the walk to the castle, go into the Craven Museum and look at the display of plans for Rowland Street to be built by Mr Thomas Duckett in 1877. Here is the answer to our ponderings over design details of the terraces. Rowland Street itself is in the middle of the development and parallel to Duckett Street, which we passed earlier. Was the street bearing the developer's name the first or the last to be built?

A variety of stones make walls, lintels and path in a Skipton ginnel.

WALK 9

MILLS AND MINES

Route: *Metherell, Cotehele, Calstock, Norris Green, Metherell (8 miles)*

Map: *OS Sheet 201 (1:50000 series)*

This is not a long walk in terms of distance, but can easily prove a very long one in terms of time, for there is an immense amount to be seen. It is centred on the west bank of the River Tamar, which separates Cornwall from Devon. Those who think of the West Country principally as a holiday area might be surprised to find that of all the regions covered in the book this area has the heaviest concentration of industrial remains. Little of this, however, is apparent at the start of the walk.

A typically Cornish lane of great antiquity, sunk between its high banks.

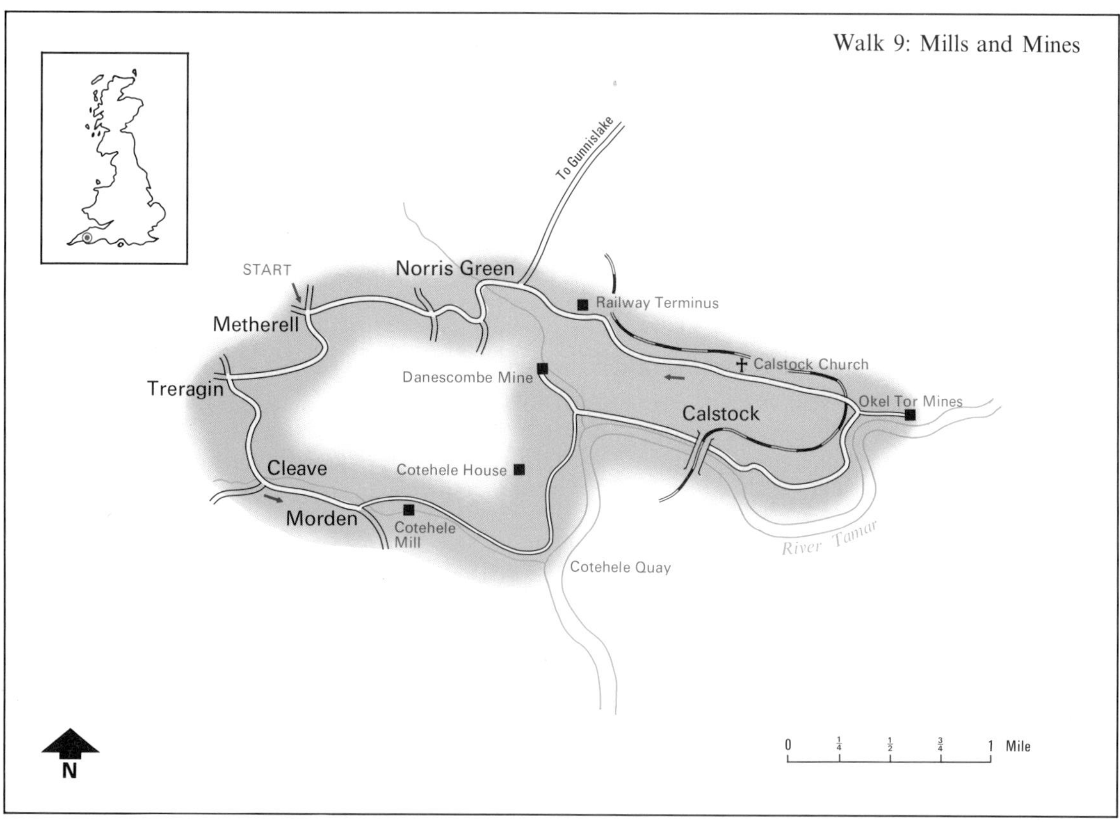

Metherell is typical of scores of small Cornish villages and hamlets. Houses are built of local granite, roofed in slate and clustered together in a tight hillside group. There are no buildings of any great architectural distinction, though the local pub claims to date back to the fourteenth century, but has been much altered over the years. First impressions are of a small agricultural community surrounded by fields and farms that creep right up to the village fringes.

The walk starts at grid reference SX 409695. Follow the lane that leads west down to the hamlet of Treragin. If Metherell is a typical small Cornish village, then this is certainly a typical Cornish lane. It winds between high banks topped with trees and hedgerows. In early summer the banks blaze with flowers. It is virtually impossible to date such lanes, whose origins may go back not merely centuries but millennia. The most that can be said with any certainty is that they predate any formal road system. Indeed, the map shows that the lanes represent purely local links between tiny settlements, which themselves dot the landscape in an apparently random fashion.

At the end of the lane turn south to make your way down towards Cleave and the wooded river valley. Already some elements of the landscape are beginning to make themselves plain. Far over to the north-west, the scene is dominated by Kit Hill, topped with a tall chimney, an announcement that prepares the way for a later scene, for the chimney was erected as a monument to Cornish miners. You also begin to see the modern break-up of the old pattern of small farms; houses are now single-family units, the former barn area having been converted into living accommodation. Another aspect of old rural life appears beside the stream that comes down the hill, heading for the Tamar. Glamorgan Mill was in use for grinding grain until quite recently. A modern concrete section is dated 1958, and the watercourse that originally supplied power to the mill is still plain to see. We shall be able to look at a water mill in more detail shortly. Here also is the first example of another local activity which still plays an important part in the economic life of the area – a market garden, with its large area of glasshouses shining out among the fields.

We now follow the little river valley east towards the Tamar. It is peaceful now, but once was an important centre of local activity. The woodland itself is mixed, and sawn stumps indicate that it was

The leat eventually arrives here, where it is carried on a wooden launder, from which it can fall onto the water-wheel of Cotehele Mill.

A saw-pit: one sawyer stands on top of the log, the other below in the pit.

once carefully managed as a valuable resource. We are now quite close to the Tamar, a navigable river of considerable importance in the past. Timber sustained the local shipbuilding industry and was also used as a building material. Morden Farm appears on the right. It is well worth pausing for a moment to look at it, for it typifies much of the style of the area. The main farmhouse is built of granite, with walls of random rubble – that is, with stones of various sizes, unshaped and not arranged in regular courses. Slate is used in the roof and this repeats what is already a familiar pattern of simple buildings using local materials. Clustered round the house are the barns and byres, scarcely different in style from the house. The steep valley side is unsuitable for crops but provides reasonable grazing for cattle. We now cross the stream on the bridge and turn through a gate on the right to join the footpath on the north bank of the stream.

The cottages by the gate suggest by their uniformity that we are now entering a different type of landscape, more formal than that of Morden Farm. This is the estate belonging to Cotehele House, which, as we shall soon see, is supporting a wide range of local activities. The first sign of things to come soon appears at the stream itself. A weir has been built across and water diverted into a

The stream near Cotehele: to the right is the weir, to the left the sluice gate controlling the flow of water down the leat.

leat controlled by sluice gates. As the stream drops down the valley, so the water in the leat remains on a higher level. Soon a path signposted to Cotehele Mill leads away to the right. The mill, house and grounds are all National Trust property. The buildings are only open during the summer, but the grounds remain open all year, so there is no problem in following the walk. A charge is made to non Trust members, but is excellent value for money. From the point of view of the walk, it is not necessary to visit Cotehele House itself, and even the mill structures can be clearly 'read' without looking inside. But few will be able to resist the temptation of a visit, so we shall give just an indication of what you will find. First, however, we can look at the outside.

Start at the point where the leat reaches the main road at the top of the mill buildings. Water from the leat falls onto the top of a large water-wheel. This is an overshot wheel, one turned by the weight of water falling into 'buckets' set on its circumference, as opposed to the more familiar undershot wheel, which is driven by the force of water against paddles set around its rim. The overshot wheel is the more efficient of the two types. It is reasonable to expect that a building such as this was used for grinding corn and this proves to be the case. Notice how maximum use is made of the mill's position. Grain can be loaded at road level. Inside the mill, it falls down through the grindstones to emerge as flour, which is then released down a chute to a waiting cart. The mill wheel is also used to power a small generator which lights the building. But the mill itself is only part of a working complex. There are also a blacksmith, wheelwright, carpenter and saddlemaker and – a very important item for this part of the world – a cider press. One other item, once a commonplace but now a rarity, is a saw-pit. A tree trunk was laid over the pit and sawn by two men, one standing above and one at the bottom of the pit. Note the oil can, used to keep the saw lubricated.

The walk continues along the road and down to the Tamar. Before crossing the bridge over the stream, turn to the right and you will see the openings for a set of lime kilns. We came across lime kilns on the Northumberland walk (page 72), but here their structure is particularly clear. At the top of the kiln is the circular opening for loading stone and coal; at the bottom you can see the aperture for shovelling out the burnt lime.

A second reason for coming here is the superb overall view of Cotehele Quay. The quay itself, with its docks, slipways and cranes, and behind it the warehouses, is a very typical small riverside development, designed for comparatively small trading vessels – coastal schooners and barges. A typical Tamar barge, *Shamrock*, can usually be seen here. Today the sailing barge may seem a romantic survivor from the age of sail, but it was in fact a prosaic working vessel. It plied up and down the river with a regular cargo not of exotic goods from distant lands but of manure for the local farms. Yet the river in its day was part of an international trading system which was already important in the ninth century, when Danish longboats came here to assist the Cornish in their fights against the Saxons. Something of the feel of the working port still lingers at Cotehele Quay, not least in its details. Look, for example, at the cast-iron bollards bearing the initials of Queen Victoria and the arrow of the War Department. They are massively built to hold large vessels. The same castings can be seen further down the Tamar at the royal dockyard of Devonport.

The way continues past and above still more lime kilns through the grounds of Cotehele House. The woodland here is still managed for its value to the estate. The way leads upwards to the house itself, a sixteenth-century house built for the Edgcumbes, who tended rather to neglect it in favour of their other residence, Mount Edgcumbe, near the mouth of the Tamar. This, from our point of view, is no bad thing, for the house retains its essential Tudor characteristics, largely unaffected by modernization and 'improvement'. The interior is splendid, but our route only takes us through the grounds and the terraces laid out between house and river. And there is quite enough here to occupy the mind. Look, for example, at the intriguing circular building with its domed roof. Its only ground-level entrance is minute and it is only when you get inside that it becomes recognizable as a dovecot, an important building for a great house, ensuring supplies of eggs and fowl. Look, too, at the river from the garden, for here it turns through an acute bend. The most prominent feature is an elegant railway viaduct, still in use, and what appear to be pathways or roadways sloping up from the river towards the hill above Calstock. Keep these features in mind for we shall be returning to them later.

The path leads down from the gardens through woodland to the Danescombe Valley, which merits exploration. Almost the first glimpse of the dark, wooded valley provides a hint that there are discoveries to be made. At the entrance is a row of cottages suggesting both by their unity of style and their isolation from the village that they are a group related to the life of the valley itself. Then as you move in you see on your left hand side a building in a rather dangerous state of ruin. It is soon apparent that it once housed water-powered machinery. There are signs of a leat behind the building, an archway over a watercourse at the front, and, in between, a large pit which once housed a water-wheel. The visible remains do not allow more than a supposition that this was a building for water-powered machines and not a grain mill. It is too low for a grain mill and the position of the wheel suggests machinery turned by horizontal shafting rather than the vertical shafts seen at Cotehele Mill. It was in fact a sawmill, but that information only appears in the written records. However, we should now be alerted to look for other signs of activity.

Walking up the valley with the stream on your right you soon discover interesting clues, starting with the large and obvious spoil heaps beyond the stream. Then a group of dwellings appears, and more clues. The first comes in the form of a house named 'Mispickel', which is an old name for the ore arsenopyrites. One of the houses is also clearly a conversion from some kind of industrial building. Put the two together, and arsenic mining begins to look likely. A little further up the path the mining theory is confirmed. A second converted industrial building appears, but here its origins are clear. This is a Cornish engine-house. It once housed a steam engine but has been converted by the Landmark Trust to house holidaymakers. Engine-houses are a familiar part of the Cornish scene, but their significance is not always easy to understand. Looking from the path, you can see to your right a ruined single-storey building from which a stone channel leads up to a chimney on the hillside. This was the boiler-house. The job of the chimney was to ensure a good updraught for the fire, and the higher it stood above the boiler the greater the draught. Here the hillside itself is used in conjunction with the chimney to provide the height.

Now the engine-house: the focal point is the wall facing south, back down the path. This is the bob wall, a massive stone construction on which the beam of the steam engine was pivoted. Inside the house was a cylinder, piston and half the beam; the rest of the beam was outside in the open air. Some engines had pump rods attached to the outside end of the beam; others had sweep arms to drive machinery. This engine seems to be one of the latter, for you can see the grooves where a flywheel turned, and the remains of buildings alongside. The engine, in fact, worked machinery for crushing ore from the mine. And the mine itself? Well, a low, wet tunnel – an adit – can be seen heading into the hillside and in front of the engine-house are the circular indentations of filled-in shafts. It is complex, because the mine was complex, working different levels at different historical periods, first for copper and then for arsenic. There is much to see in this little valley and you could spend a week here without uncovering all its secrets. But we shall return to the roadway by the Tamar.

We pass a very attractive, veranda'ed building, the Danescombe Valley Hotel, beyond which are yet more lime kilns. There are also boat-yards, for this was once an important boat-building centre. But now is the time to recollect the view from the Cotehele woods. A stone bridge straddles the roadway, and its angle makes it plain that it carried one of those slanting paths down towards the river; the second sloping path appears beyond it on the left. The puzzle is not yet solved, but another piece has been put into place.

Soon, however, our attention is caught by the great Calstock viaduct across the river. You can still see the signs of the ferry it supplanted in the roadway down to the river on the opposite bank. But what of the viaduct itself? We are accustomed to seeing great examples of Victorian engineering, but this viaduct is not quite what it appears. The building material is the giveaway – not stone, as it appears from a distance, but concrete. It is not in fact nineteenth-century at all, but a twentieth-century structure and you can still find traces of one unusual feature. At the nearside you can see a concrete plinth, above which iron brackets can be seen

Cotehele Quay with the Tamar barge *Shamrock*.

A naval cast-iron bollard, identified by the royal initials and War Department mark, that found its way to Cotehele Quay.

The birds give the clue to the function of the circular stone building: the dovecot at Cotehele House.

The majestic Calstock viaduct, built in this century in concrete blocks, not stone.

standing out from the parapet. These are the remains of a waggon hoist, a vertical lift that carried trucks between the railway above and the quay below.

Calstock itself was once a thriving inland port and industrial centre, and traces of the past remain in old house names, such as the Steam Packet, once an inn for travellers by river steamer. The village is squeezed and restricted by its location so that it seems almost to threaten to tumble down its narrow streets and alleys to the river. It is a village full of delightful details. Look, for example, at the boots of the Boot Inn sign, which you walk past to follow Harewood Road. Note the orchard behind its high walls, a second reminder that we are in cider country. The walk continues on a footpath, a narrow track above the Tamar, which forks off to the right where Harewood Road joins Eric Road. It offers splendid views of the reed-fringed river with its high, protective flood banks, and a glimpse of distant – and somewhat drunken-looking – mine chimneys. Then you arrive at Okel Tor quay and the remains of Okel Tor mines (grid reference 447688).

The nature of the mines is evident from the surrounding area. Although the surface buildings are in ruins, indicating that many years have passed since work ended, the spoil heaps are still almost bare of vegetation and only the toughest plants – heathers and gorses – now grow. This suggests arsenic mining, which was indeed an important part of the work here, though in earlier times the mine was also worked for tin and copper. Among the remains, very overgrown by dense and prickly gorses, it is possible to discern the arsenic flues. The ore was heated and the waste gases passed down these long flues, in which the arsenic condensed. The main flues can be found on the uphill side of the site, leading off towards a distant chimney. Arsenic was widely used in the glass industry, in the manufacture of enamels, and, as all readers of detective stories know, in insecticides and other poisons.

Retrace your steps and take the path up to the prominent stack beside the road, where you will find an engine-house and – to be treated with extreme caution – the old shaft. On rejoining the road take the left-hand turn across the railway at the level crossing. This is an ungated crossing, which tells you something about the line, especially when put together with the concrete used for Calstock viaduct. The viaduct suggests a late construction date and the ungated crossing tells us that this was probably a light railway built following the Light Railway Act of 1896. This Act allowed companies to provide railways on the cheap to serve the less populous and less prosperous areas – railways built for slower, lighter trains than those of the main line, and with less rigorous safety standards, hence the absence of gates. This particular line from Calstock to Bere Alston was authorized in 1900. We shall find out a little more about it later. For the time being note the wooden slats which stop animals straying up the line, and the stop sign for train drivers who have to pause at the crossing.

The road now curves round to give a view of another loop of the river and a glimpse of the fine open-air museum of Morwellham before we arrive at Calstock church. The latter is something of a mystery. The town is now far below us on the riverside, so why is the church here, in isolation, at the top of the hill? The church itself, like so many parish churches, bears the marks of many alterations made through the centuries, notably those of the Victorian restorers whose heavy hands descended on many hapless buildings. The earliest part is the central aisle, with fourteenth-century granite pillars on the north side. Other parts can be dated quite accurately. The Edgcumbe chapel, added by the Edgcumbes of Cotehele, was built in 1558, and a splendid eighteenth-century painting of bell-ringers informs us that the bells were cast in 1773 and lists fines for numerous offences, from marring a peal to wearing spurs in church. All this speaks of a church as a centre of continuing importance to the community, but why so far away? It can only be conjecture, but it seems probable that when the church was first consecrated the original village was that of an agricultural community centred up here on the hillside. The development of mining and the increased river trade shifted the community down to its present position by the river. The area around here is known as Churchtown and the surrounding buildings are of considerable age, which gives solid support to the theory. However, the church has still more information to provide, for the churchyard has a great deal to say about local conditions in the last century. Here you will find memorials to those killed in mining accidents, including a stone to Isaac Sleep, 'Who was accidentally killed in Virtuous-Lady Mine by the crank of the water wheel, the 19th of August 1831, aged 14 years'. It is signed by the mason – T. Sleep.

From the church follow the road beside the railway and take the fork to the left toward Norris Green. At the crossroads is a most interesting group of buildings. Here we have yet another mine and a very typical group of engine-houses. You will often find engine-houses in groups of two and occasionally three. The largest house held the biggest engine, the pumping engine; the smaller

This was once the terminus of the East Cornwall Mineral Railway. The overgrown building on the left was the engine shed, the tower held a water tank and where the car now stands was a turntable for locomotives.

The ruins of an engine-house, with its ivy-covered chimney.

house held a whim or winding engine, used to draw ore and men up and down the shaft; and the third house, where there was one, housed a stamps engine for crushing the ore. A century ago there were 272 pumping engines, 184 whim engines and 70 stamps engines in Cornwall. Alongside the mine the road crosses a disused railway – and it is here that we can put in the last piece of our railway puzzle. This line came down from the north following a similar route to the present line – which in fact it joined – but here comes to a dead end at a group of buildings on the top of the hill above the river. You can see the old engine shed, a turntable, water tower and a third building on the very brink of the hill. What we see is the remains of the East Cornwall Mineral Railway which served the local mines. A glance at the map will confirm that we are standing above the sloping path we first saw from Cotehele. In other words, a conventional railway reached this point, after which the trucks continued on downhill on the inclined plane, while locomotives were turned on the turntable for the return journey. When the light railway was built, the incline was no longer needed. Railway enthusiasts might also like to note that the mineral line here was narrow-gauge, converted to standard-gauge for the new route.

The walk continues down the hill to Norris Green, with views across the wooded Danescombe Valley. The world of mines is left behind and we are back with the farms. Here you can still see signs of old trackways such as that leading up the side of the farm wall at the bottom of the hill and the green lane that runs up off the road to the right. Look out, too, for the farm cottage where a pair of buttresses form both supports and a porchway. At the top of the hill there is an interesting farm group centred on a long house where farmhouse and cowhouse are part of the same long building. Here we turn right and follow the lane back to the peaceful village of Metherell.

WALK 10

Gunpowder Plots

Route: *Faversham, Oare, Faversham (5 miles)*
Maps: *OS Sheet 178 (1:50 000 series) and Faversham street plan*

In our walks so far we have taken an area of the country and started by looking at the lie of the landscape or at the effects of progress on an area. In Faversham, however, we had heard of a specific industry which we wanted to trace. In 1969 The Faversham Society started to restore the Chart Gunpowder Mills and so far have succeeded in renovating one mill nearly to working order. The mills themselves are in the middle of a modern housing estate and seem like an oasis in a desert of recent development. Up until 1934 Faversham produced an enormous amount of munitions, so the aim of this walk is to explore what is left of this vast industry, which must have been larger than the remaining Chart Mills site.

The cark park at the centre of Faversham is large and an unusual shape. Close by are a newly built health centre and a swimming pool. It makes one wonder what was cleared to make such an area in the centre of a town. In the middle is the Arden Theatre, a new lease of life given to an old warehouse. There are several alleys, shops on the circumference and the arch of an old coaching inn. One path is marked 'Chart Gunpowder Mills' but instead of rushing directly to our objective we will start by following a short alley to West Street. The first part of the street has been paved and a series of old, mainly unspoiled shop fronts lead from the Guildhall. These have sixteenth- and seventeenth-century origins and as such make up a part of the older core of the town. Across South Road this style of older buildings is still evident, with gaps where industry has intruded in the form of a fertilizer merchant and the old gasworks, still with a gasholder. Just why they are here, despite the narrow road access, is for the moment unclear. Here also are some very pleasant cottages with shutters and projecting upper storeys, or jetties. In fact the whole area to the left is full of little streets with such houses. At the end of West Street the road widens to a triangle with a nineteenth-century brick warehouse on one side. Opposite is Tanners Street, possibly giving a clue to an earlier occupation. The tanning of leather requires a good deal of water, and just past the warehouse is Stonebridge Pond. The pond is a very picturesque corner of Faversham with its gardens, allotments, ducks and weatherboarded houses – a rural piece of the town contrasting with the high-density housing we have just left. However, there is something more to Stonebridge Pond than just an area of water. The gardens and allotments are divided by a series of channels, rather like an ornamental water-garden, with little bridges connecting the stretches of land. It is all rather puzzling.

On the other side of the road a sign points down a path to the Chart Mills. A stream runs alongside the path and the adjoining Millstream Close gives a clue to its use. There are signs of culverting and channelling and we pass Nobel Court, a hint of what is to come, for Nobel, of Nobel Prize fame, made his fortune by the invention of blasting gelatine, which was made in the town. Finally we arrive at Chart Mills. Here chemicals were ground to powder by two large vertical stone wheels trundling round on a horizontal bedstone. This mill used a breast-shot water-wheel, and to avoid the risk of sparks all the internal cogs were made of wood. Most of the long walls and the roof were of timber construction, with brick

Watercourses, cogs and bedstone with the partially restored Chart Gunpowder Mill in the background.

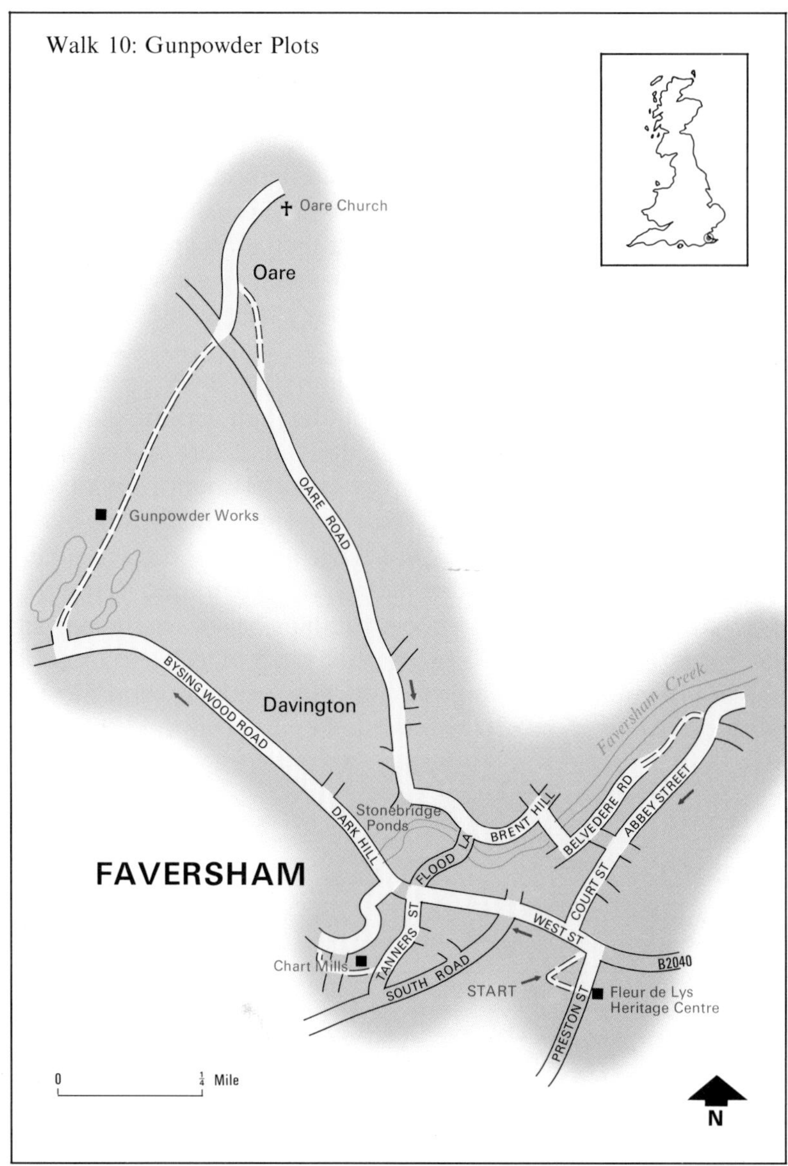

end walls, so that in the event of an accident – a not unusual occurrence – the blast would be channelled where damage would be minimal. The surrounding trees were also planted to localize damage. A postcard in the mill shows a load of powder being carried in a punt, a much safer method than carrying it in open carts with iron-shod wheels. This latter practice was forbidden by a by-law of 1742.

The route now runs past further sets of bedstones into Cress Way and returns to Stonebridge Pond. It then continues left up Dark Hill, signposted to Luddenham. On the right, past a thatched gazebo, the ground falls away sharply. The area has been quarried, but for what is not evident. Later research showed this to be the terminus of the Davington Light Railway, a private line used to take people to work at later gunpowder factories. As explosives became more powerful, safety demanded that the danger should be removed from the town. The sheds now being used in the quarry yard are recognizable in old photographs as station buildings. Like the Chart Mills, this is a piece of the past surrounded by a modern housing estate. There are footpaths which might follow the line of the railway but as these are unclear we follow a route down Bysing Wood Road. Looking around this estate one might be anywhere. A similar feeling occurs in a modern shopping precinct – with the same names over the shops, the same goods for sale. So often on our walks we have noted local variations in planning, materials and adaptation to difficulties, such as building on a hillside, but the modern estate is the same wherever you are. At the end of the estate on the left there are signs of earthworks: large areas of the surface clay have been cleared. This suggests a brickworks, and indeed brick kilns can be found nearby.

On the right, by the road sign marking the end of the speed limit, stands a large wall, and the route turns through a pair of old gate piers. One of the ingredients of gunpowder is charcoal and the first thing we notice is that the trees have been coppiced and, to judge by the stumps, some of them for a long time. This track marks the start of the Oare Works, which were in operation by 1719. On a rise above the path is a fine utilitarian house, built presumably for a works manager, and on the right are brick sheds

Well hidden in the undergrowth is an overflow for the gunpowder works' canal system.

of a later era. The trees all around were planted as blast barriers as at Chart Mills, leaving a fine heritage.

The manufacture of explosives has several requirements: chemicals, which need processing; water, to be used in the cooling process as well as for motive power and transport (we have already come across a second transport system, a light railway); wood for charcoal, which we have seen; and places to carry out these processes and store the finished goods.

Further along the path we soon come across signs of building. Set into the hillside is a cavern-shaped wall of brick. Here the track veers to the right and crosses a stream on a brick-arched bridge. Steps lead down to a little quay, in an integrated style very reminiscent of the type of engineering found on canals. There are indications that the stream has indeed been canalized and, as it was presumably used for transport, it seems sensible to follow it to see where it leads. An area like this needs to be explored, so use the waterway as a base and search for clues on either side. Almost immediately we find another building with flues and fireplaces. There are signs of a more complex process than the simple grinding of powder, suggesting that this dates from the time when gunpowder had given way to gun cotton and other explosives such as TNT, which were more complicated to make. Blocks for mounting machinery can be seen and in the nearby undergrowth there is an overflow sluice, complete with its wooden trough. A little further on the remains of another bridge covered in ivy lead to a path following the waterway, again reminiscent of a canal towpath. Round a corner the remains of a large industrial working suddenly appears. It is impossible to say exactly what went on here but various features are worth noting. The waterway terminates in a wharf. There is a sluice to take away excess water, and a kiln with a long flue. The area is divided by a large blast wall with sloping grooves, presumably to hold a roof structure, and more holes and bolt plates for machinery. Climbing the earthworks on either side gives one an idea of the vast construction needed for the building.

Further exploration reveals watercourses of a familiar shape, and a further complex with thick walls and a repeated pattern of building which could have been stores. Back on the original main track there is a view past gravel pits towards Dark Hill and the light railway terminus; a straight level path may be the track-bed; by the fork to a water mill, there is a concrete box with a step at one end – possibly a platform?

The mill itself is an attractive building with signs of a wheel and beyond it stand workers' cottages. From here one can see the

Part of the gunpowder works hidden in the woods.

hamlet of Oare and its creek, which is where the mill stream – and thus, we suspect, the excess water from the gunpowder works – flows to the sea. At Oare crossroads the route takes the road signposted to Harty Ferry past The Three Mariners pub. From Oare church, perched on high ground, there is a view of the creek, packed with boats, including a small coaster. The church itself has a small shingled spire, a west door dated by Pevsner as thirteenth-century and a crown post roof. Inside the church, a plaque on the north wall commemorates the death of Oare parishioners killed in a gunpowder explosion in 1916. On the way back to Oare crossroads there is much to see in the panorama. A mile and a quarter away to the south-east is the spire of St Mary's, Faversham, unusually constructed on four flying buttresses. At about that distance, and slightly to its right, is a brick tower windmill. A clear level track emerges from the head of Oare Creek, disappears under the road and reappears on the other side towards Uplees, to the north-west. This is the track of the light railway. (The Uplees terminus, where there is an old engine-shed and remains of a station, and large square blockhouses on the marsh, which, until recently, were lead-lined and used to store nitroglycerine, merit a separate exploration.)

From the footpath from the Harty Ferry road to the head of the creek it is possible to see the tunnel, dated 1916, which takes the line under the road and a piece of railway track, as well as a now redundant warning sign saying 'trains crossing'. Our road back to Faversham passes the tower mill. Now converted to a dwelling, it still has its staging, or balcony, and it is clear where the rotating cap carrying the sails was. In fact the adjacent pub sign is a nearly accurate picture of how the windmill would have looked with its sails. On either side of the road there are extensive gravel workings and hints of brickworks before the road rises to Davington. Now part of Faversham, Davington is noted for its priory. Although most of the priory apart from the church is in private hands, much of the old building remains, since it was bought in 1845 by an artist called Thomas Willement and restored as a private house. There is also a school with an outside bell and cannons used as bollards. Following the priory wall to the left, you pass a doorway with a spyhole. Stonebridge Pond is below.

Our first look at the pond left us uncertain of its purpose. Since then we have discovered more about the gunpowder industry and the importance of the pond is now clearer. First there is a layout of waterways similar to that around the Oare Works. The water ends in Faversham Creek, as did the previous stream in Oare Creek. From an earlier map it is obvious that two natural streams were used for this work so there must have been a constant flow of water.

The one necessity of the industry we have not considered is the raw materials: saltpetre, sulphur and charcoal. These were not available locally, and the creeks provided a means of transport for importing them and also exporting the finished product. By the creek is a brick wall of similar design to the one at Chart Mills. We were later told of bedstones and a surviving wheel-pit in the private allotments. Clearly the pond was a reservoir and the water divided to supply mills. All this area was the Home Works, worked as early as 1653 by one Daniel Judd and closed in 1934. Cress Way marked the upper reservoir for the Chart Mills, and was used later for growing cress. In Jacob's *History of Faversham* of 1774 the author notes: 'The only considerable manufacture carried on here is of that dreadful composition gunpowder prepared by water and horse mills.' He records eleven sets of water and six of horse-powered mills. Thus, from knowing of the existence of one restored mill, the detective has uncovered the remains of a vast industry.

Was Jacob's 'considerable manufacture' all Faversham has to offer? There is more of the town to see and our immediate attention was caught by a considerable amount of rigging. The route continues down Brent Hill to the head of the creek. The lane branching back to West Street is called Flood Lane and this little area is well worth exploring. There are gateposts and a building overlooking the quay in the same style as the gunpowder mill's end wall. Tied up in the creek was a two-masted sailing barge. Across the creek is the frontage belonging to the West Street fertilizer works, thus explaining their position on that narrow

A timber-framed warehouse still in use on Standard Quay in Faversham.

Part of the charm of the Standard Quay warehouse is the pattern of brick infill, or nogging.

A spritsail barge at the top of Faversham creek. On the right is a wall which is of the same type as can be seen in gunpowder factory remains.

street. As the creek continues round the corner, an imposing Georgian building catches the eye. This is the old customs house, now a private house with a fine view over the creek.

The creek, running down to the sea, is full of boats of all sizes and is lined on one side with buildings that still bustle with life. It also contrasts well with Walberswick, being an industrial rather than a fishing area. Crossing the creek is a swing bridge complete with a hut for the control gear, and underneath the bridge a set of gates which, when closed, keep a level of water in the upper creek, necessary as this part is tidal. Across the bridge is a winch, curiously set at ninety degrees to the roadway, which suggests that it was used to operate the bridge. Just beyond the bridge is a timber-framed building called T/S *Hasarde*. Set by the creek, it must have been used as warehousing of some sort, and the size of the supporting timbers suggests that the ground floor might have been open. Looking it up later revealed that it was the town's fish market and store. It has been superbly restored and the reason for its name lies with its use as the headquarters of the local Sea Scouts. It is interesting to contrast it with the Faversham Boxing Club's hall next door, which was purpose-built in 1911.

Our route is down Belvedere Road, the access road for the warehouses adjoining the creek. Here the feeling is very much one of serious work for all the buildings are in use. Though no longer served by the creek, the old timber yard still survives. The road turns into a path that has a 'feel' about it. There are no obvious clues yet, but something about the line of the path, the width and the juxtapositioning of the buildings seems to say 'railway'. The surface is concrete and no railway remains are in evidence until, nearing the water again, you see sleepers and a wooden gate fence of distinct railway design. The map shows the space to have contained sidings looping right round the town, joining the main line some distance away. Another chance for exploration.

Back at the creek at Standard Quay is an interesting set of buildings. First a long, low building. Inside, the substantial timber frame is clearly visible, with partitions dividing the space. At one point a large round pillar is incorporated in the structure – it might easily have been cut from a ship's mast. The timber frame has been infilled by brick nogging in a variety of shapes. Opposite there are several fine weatherboarded warehouses on a stone base, again still in use. Further down the creek, past the remains of a barge, is a black nineteenth-century warehouse with a gantry for an overhead hoist over the creek. It looks almost two-dimensional against the flat marshland. In faint lettering it is possible to make out the words 'Faversham Oyster Company' – another alternative industry to gunpowder. The route passes the Elizabethan warehouse, goes along Abbey Road and turns right into Abbey Street. At the turn, don't miss the two medieval barns straight ahead at Abbey Farm.

The first thing to note about Abbey Street is the overall impact. The street widens towards the town hall and there are trees at points in the pavement. A lack of telegraph poles and a certain uniformity of design point to an overall conservation scheme. (There was one in 1961, which rescued many of the buildings.) Notice the mix at the creek end, with industry and new houses appearing among the old. The architect of the modern terrace has tried to echo the lines of the older houses in the street without producing a mock period look. The street has a wealth of architectural detail. There are windows of all periods, from medieval onwards. Older timber frames have had later fronts added. There is a variety of doorways, columns, cornices, carvings, badges, heads, gables, jetties and levels. Number 89 posed a puzzle. The ground-floor walls are made to look grander by having the appearance of ashlar stone. This is a common occurrence and is usually done in stucco over-rendering. Here,

Number 89 Abbey Street shows exposed timber-frame construction with characteristic window gaps. The ground floor is also wood but made to look like ashlar stone.

Classic timber-framed houses showing their jetties, or overhangs.

however, the wall edges were chamfered and there were signs of a peg. It transpired that the 'mock' in this case was wood. One building in Abbey Street demands special attention, and that is number 80. Besides the medieval barns at Abbey Farm, number 80 is the only other substantial building of that period in this part of the street. Later research reveals that part of the building adjoins the remains of the abbey gate, of which, like the abbey itself, virtually nothing is left. The house was converted by a former mayor of Faversham, Thomas Arden, a man remembered as the subject of the Elizabethan play *Arden of Faversham*.

Abbey Street turns into Court Street with two rival breweries, one on each side of the road. As the street gets wider the buildings here get grander, as befits the town centre. Past the town pump is the Guildhall, on stilts, still hosting a market. At the side of the

The wooden pillars supporting Faversham's Guildhall leave room for a market underneath.

Guildhall is a fine row of shops, especially the chemist's with its pestle and mortar outside and old shop fittings inside. There are still archways, alleys and courtyards worth looking at. Partridge Lane in particular has a fine medieval building. The large overhang is supported on pillars, creating a large space underneath which could have been used as a merchant's premises.

Turn down Preston Street past the modern carved shop front to a street full of mostly mundane buildings, with one exception. This is the Fleur de Lys, run by the Faversham Society as a heritage centre. The buildings and exhibitions are well worth a visit. One impressive detail is the patterned cast-iron roof supports in the much later meeting-room at the back. At the Fleur de Lys many of the unknowns can be made known and theories confirmed or rejected.

Although the specific purpose of this walk was to examine the gunpowder industry, there is an abundance of other material to detect and enjoy.

WALK 11

FORMER GLORIES

Route: *The walk is round the town of Abingdon starting at Rye Farm car park off the A415 immediately south of the bridge (4 miles)*

Maps: *OS Sheet 164 (1:50 000 series) and Abingdon street plan*

In some ways Abingdon is a similar town to Faversham. Both are about the same size, both had substantial abbeys before the Dissolution, both have a raised town hall. Here the similarity ends. Abingdon has experienced prosperity and decline, and this walk offers an opportunity to explore not only bricks and mortar but also the social history of the town and its community.

Leave the car park and walk along the raised pavement beside the modern main road towards the bridge. South of the river there are virtually no buildings to be seen. Any river, especially one as powerful as the Thames, can overflow its banks, hence the need for a raised causeway. However, on the north side of the river the houses come right down to the water's edge and judging by the eye they seem to be on higher ground. It seems clear that when the river floods water spreads to the south rather than to the north, but at present it is not clear whether this is due to the natural lie of the land or man's intervention.

From the bridge there is much to see. First the river itself. In the distance, to the east, there is a lock, which shows that the river is navigable. Now it caters for holiday traffic, but once it was a commercial waterway, and we will look for clues to that commercial past. The water is divided by islands and the bridge does not cross in a single span but by a number of narrow arches with one broad arch in the centre. The smaller arches are pointed while the main arch traces a segment of a circle – pointed arches suggest antiquity, but the wider span is of more modern date. A new hotel stands on a flattened island. Was this levelled to make the car park or was there something here before the hotel? Certainly the little accommodation bridge must have been there before the isolated hotel block, as it is constructed of older brick. To the north of the island, the waterway has a different character from that of the main flow. Water enters the river through two tunnels which look like mill races, though the adjacent street name, Thames Street, offers no clue.

Standing by the bridge looking towards the town you can see to your left a small terrace of houses parallel to the river. The road curves gently up towards the town and is lined with shops, behind which is a large building consisting of a central hexagonal block with two wings. Its solidity and the large number of very small windows suggest a prison, and on reaching the entrance you will see the name 'The Old Gaol'. Next to the entrance gate is an imposing ashlar-fronted building now used by the planning department. Next door is the county police station. This is something of a puzzle. Abingdon is now in Oxfordshire and Oxford is the county town and always has been. Local government reorganization changed the county boundaries and Abingdon was previously in Berkshire – but Reading is the county town for Berkshire. It does seem to be a slight mystery.

The presence of a gaol of this size suggests a town of some importance. The gaol itself was built at the beginning of the nineteenth century and its inmates included prisoners from the Napoleonic Wars. It is well worth visiting. There is a central tower with a spiral staircase and the conversion of the building to a sports

Warehouses and the gaol have both now found different uses.

centre has not destroyed its character. Note how walls not exposed to public view are made from cheaper, undressed stone.

The rest of Bridge Street is a mix of buildings. On one of them faint traces of writing proclaim that it was once the Abingdon Liberal Club. At one point various smaller old properties have been knocked together to make a single shop with a modern ground-floor front. It is important for the townscape detective to look above the ground floor. As trading is normally a ground-floor activity, that is where development tends to happen. The upper floors here appear to contain some living areas, though those above the larger shops no longer show any signs of domestic use and seem to be used for offices and storage. The one exception is the little newsagent which is still a family business; the rooms above are clearly lived in.

At the top of Bridge Street is the Market Square, dominated by the county hall, with space underneath for a market. It was built about 1680 by Christopher Kempster, who worked with Sir Christopher Wren. The first floor houses the town's museum. There is a wide staircase to mount in the windowless tower built at the back, and the stairs also go down to a basement. The tower is in fact topped by a header tank, which until relatively recently was part of the town's water supply. The water was pumped by a gas engine which is still there in the basement (it is of the same design and manufacture as the engine at the George Leatt Museum in Skipton). Beneath the arches, the high, thick stone supports seem in much grander style than the wooden pillars of Faversham's town hall. It was in fact built almost exactly a hundred years later and its design shows a greater degree of prosperity, as do the materials used – though this may reflect little more than the greater availability of stone in Berkshire than in Kent.

From the steps in front of the county hall there is much to see.

A small mullioned window in East St Helen Street.

First there is the Church of St Nicolas, with its Norman doorway, abutting a large arched gateway. The gateway itself has ecclesiastical windows, a figure in a decorated niche and crests above the arch. The church and the market-place are both on the town side of the arch. This is typical of the layout found outside the walls of an important abbey or monastery. On the far side of the arch is a group of official-looking municipal buildings in a hotchpotch of styles and materials. This sort of group demands careful inspection, and is described in more detail on page 207. Thanks to the market, the square itself has survived and there are some interesting buildings surrounding it.

Looking down the High Street is a pleasure. There are the usual grand fronts with plastic signs but many of the shops are well cared for, especially those owned locally. Building societies and other national bodies implant their corporate image, but the changes are often only transient – again they do not affect the first floors. Here the details abound. A more serious intrusion into the old town can be seen in the view across the square. There is a shopping precinct and, to the right, a stretch of buildings ending in the Queen's Hotel. This has an odd appearance, for it is badly proportioned and seems to be two quite different buildings stuck together. Old photographs show that the left-hand side, now altered, was part of the old Queen's Hotel, while the right-hand side was formerly a printer's shop.

Between the county hall and the end of East St Helen Street is a small group of medieval buildings, hidden from view by the mass of the county hall. Perhaps they have survived because they are hidden, and so have escaped commercial pressures. Jutting out from the tourist board offices is part of the original structural timber frame.

East St Helen Street is still referred to by older locals as 'Fore Street', while West St Helen Street was 'Back Street'. 'Fore Street' means principal street, and East St Helen Street has certainly been in use for a very long time. It connects a slipway on the river with the start of the old Oxford road. All the large houses are to the left, their covered archways giving the appearance of a line of coaching inns. However, access was required not for coaches carrying people but for carts carying goods to the river, for these were merchants' houses. Like Abbey Street in Faversham, this street developed from its position by the water.

The street is too narrow to be a market street and runs in a gentle curve which keeps the end of the street as a surprise. As in Abbey Street, there is a wealth of material for the architect

It is tempting to call this an eighteenth-century house from its front, but the side tells another story.

detective. However, here the detection is not so much in spotting individual items but tracing the history of the houses. On the left is number 26. From its overhang and gables it seems to have been built in the late fifteenth century. If you look more closely you will see decorated medieval windows in the side of the gables. Twickenham House with its fine front door and stable block is mid-Georgian. Number 30 also has a Georgian look with a splendid door, but the side of the building is quite different, with brick giving way to rubble walling and the roof becoming steeper – a much earlier style. There are other signs of change in East St Helen Street: storeys have been added; where brick and render frontages abut, the brick front is not aligned with the render but further forward. Number 28, despite its Georgian doorway, is of stone and timber construction, revealing it to be much earlier. One wonders if there was rivalry between the owners of the three grand pediments. How many of these rendered fronts, including mock ashlar again but not in wood, hide earlier timber frames? For example, can number 57, with its decorations and initials 'R.E.', really date from the stated 1732?

Over the roofs the spire of St Helen's Church is visible. Before the church comes into view there is a small development called Fairlawn Wharf. The main building is directly on the water's edge and has low arches for access to boats. This is the first positive sign of commercial use of the Thames. Then, as the street widens, the church itself comes into view. The pulpit of 1636 is particularly noteworthy; unfortunately it was 'altered' when the Victorian screen was erected. In the Lady chapel roof a series of medieval painted panels represent the Tree of Jesse. Looking around, you can see that the church is as wide as it is long.

The churchyard is bounded by almshouses. The main row has a covered walk running along it. The cupola in the centre of the roof surmounts a hall where the governors of the charity, Christ's Hospital, still meet regularly. The room, which is panelled and hung with portraits of the benefactors, revealed two clues. The first was a poem written about the building of Abingdon Bridge. It is impossible to read in the original but a transcript shows the author to be an early McGonagall:

> King Henry the Fifth in his fourth yere
> He hath i found for his folke a bridge in Berkeshire
> For cartis and carriage many goo and come clere
> That many Wynters afore were marred in the myre.

Rough though the dating is, it seems to match our earlier thoughts about the bridge, and confirms Abingdon as originally having been in Berkshire. The other clue was a painting of Abingdon's waterfront which clearly shows another stone bridge with several arches.

Continuing through the churchyard and taking due note of the improving texts on the almshouse wall, we reach the river. This is

The cast-iron bridge built by the Wilts and Berks Canal Company to span the River Ock.

a very pretty spot with a good view of Abingdon Bridge. The almshouses continue along the front but in the middle of the group of buildings is the Old Anchor Inn. Inside the pub a photograph on the wall shows the pub in earlier days, and, tied up on the wharf outside, a canal narrowboat. Outside, looking west along the wharf, there is no sign of the stone bridge we saw in the almshouse painting; instead there is a splendid cast-iron one over the River Ock. An inscription informs us that it was cast by Acramans of Bristol for the Wilts and Berks Canal Company. The bridge is too low for a canal boat to pass underneath but farther along the Thames by Wharf Close a warehouse and an indentation in the bank mark the start of the now derelict canal. It is still possible to follow its course from Caldecott Road – another project for the landscape detective.

Follow the path to the east side of the stream, which gives a fine view of the back of the almshouses, till you reach a large, newly converted building, St Helen's Mill. From here a path leads back through the churchyard to West St Helen Street. As you walk it is worth reading the stone plaques on the almshouses – they belong to a time when charity began at home. Through the arch and on the left a footpath at the side of the churchyard leads west through a housing estate. It was obviously planned as one unit, and a considerable area of the town must have been cleared at one go. The path crosses the Ock by a wooden footbridge. There is a back view of the mill and a waterfall where two streams become one. The river has been divided on two levels, probably to provide the power to drive the mill, but as neither stream passes near the building they must have been diverted at a later date. A low arch still visible at the side of the mill indicates the probable original course of the mill stream.

The path continues as a pleasant country walk. On the left, meadows, fenced down to the water, provide grazing for animals. However, these are ominously ringed with new building, which makes one wonder whether the land will survive as pasture. On the right across the stream is a group of industrial buildings. The layout is typical of a tower brewery, in which water – or 'liquor', as it is called in the trade – is pumped to the top and taken through the brewing process by gravity.

The path itself continues along the piece of land between the streams. Unsuitable for other use, a park has been created. Most of the vegetation has been left intentionally as a wilderness but a line of willows, regimented and close together, points to positive forestry. Halfway along the path an overflow links the two streams.

There are remains of sluices and culverts in the lower levels but nothing to indicate their purpose. At this point houses and gardens line the streams as new estates have been built. On the left the gardens are very long, suggesting that grazing land has been sold in strips to the householders. On the right is a block of council flats and between these and the stream a set of low, old industrial buildings, in places very like those of the brewery we have just passed. On an old map these are marked as part of a malt-house complex. Then another multi-arched stone bridge comes into view. The layout of the meadows makes it possible to look at the bridge in detail, because some of the arches are now stranded on dry land. The shape of the arches indicates that this is an old bridge and if you look at more than one of these you will see how the bridge has been widened and find some of the original stone supporting ribs.

Although it is tempting to search the area to the left of the bridge for signs of the canal, as it surely passed close by, our route turns right over the bridge. From the bridge the stream continues through meadows. To the left there are signs of the town's later industry. A large industrial area turns out to be the old MG factory, the honest brick buildings lost behind trading estate cladding. At the end of the bridge a little house with cast-iron windows heralds the beginning of Ock Street, which shares its name with the stream we have been following.

Here is a Victorian development with a terrace of houses and a small industrial site. Along Spring Road is an interesting development of stone buildings around Winterborne Road. They have

Various stages of building can be seen by looking underneath the Ock bridge.

curious details in mouldings and windows. However, these are not very old. The area, together with Spring Terrace, was developed by a local builder, Mr Winterborne. Spring Terrace is a strange edifice – a terrace of houses sideways on to the road with a balcony running its entire length at front-door level. It looks rather like a colonial hotel, and one story is that it was built as Abingdon Station Hotel. However, there are no signs of a railway. Our route crosses Spring Road and continues through a park, a good example of a Victorian park with its bowling green and the obligatory statue of Prince Albert. How different this is from the present municipal idea of the recreational area we saw along the Ock Walk!

The partially hidden Abingdon conduit.

The Railway Inn's sign shows a broad-gauge GWR engine and the old Abingdon station.

Close to the buildings of Abingdon School there is a small stone structure with a locked door, behind which one can detect the sound of running water. From here, names give repeated clues as we enter Conduit Road, past Carswell School to almshouses with a niche in their side wall. Later research showed the conduit to be in existence in 1554 as a source of the town's water. Carrswell, or 'clear well', was a small natural well, and in 1799 the sum of £6 was 'allowed to Mr Richard Ely towards repairing and beautifying the Carrswell'. The niche held the drinking fountain and bears his name and the date. As a prominent person in the town, could he be 'R.E.' of 59 East St Helen Street?

Back towards the centre of town, past the brewery's mock-Tudor cottages, there are two sad buildings. The first is an empty uncared-for house in front of the classical-looking columned Baptist church. This stands opposite an early Georgian house complete with courtyard and stables, described by Pevsner as 'the grandest house in Abingdon' but, when we saw it, covered in scaffolding, its gates demolished and the skeleton of a modern office complex attached to the rear. This is one of many office developments to be seen in the town, and shows the immense social contrast with Faversham, which retains a much more mundane mix of trade, industry and dwelling.

At the east end of the stableyard there is a fascinating later addition to the building. Under a large oriel window are three carved heads and the words 'The Beaconsfield'. Clearly the profiles are of worthy gentlemen, one of whom is recognizable as Disraeli, ennobled as Viscount Beaconsfield. This was in fact the local branch of his national social club, the Primrose League.

Reaching The Square, which is not a square, we also reach the other end of the High Street. The 1930s cinema adds an honest touch to the respectable Victorian buildings one usually finds in such a position. Adding a bit of fun to the sombre upright banks is a well built row of shops decorated with curls, frills and a pagoda style of roof, part of which is appropriately a Chinese take-away.

Our route takes us up Bath Street as far as the fine Stratton House, then turns right to a subway under a new road, Stratton Way. On both sides of the modern road there are signs of a garden: stone walls, trees and niches form almost a modern folly. The sides of the houses show with what brutality the new road was forged. Farther up Bath Street a warehouse with a crane attached now serves as workshops for Abingdon School; there is no indication of its original use. Passing imposing buildings and gateways, the route turns right up an alley, through an estate to a large expanse of grass. A plaque tells us that is the site of Fitzharry's Manor.

Modern housing estates require expanses of land which are hard to find in built-up areas. One common method of acquiring space is by demolishing a grand house with substantial grounds. Abingdon has at least three such estates. This is one. Another, which we saw from the Ock Walk, is built in the grounds of Caldecott House (the sluices there were part of the water gardens). The third is Barton Court estate, which is not on the walk but is worth a visit to see how the small amount of remaining ruin dominates the modern houses.

At the end of a green on this estate is a mound surrounded by a depression, called the Motte. For some time we believed that this was part of the mansion's garden landscape, and were sceptical of the official version. However, documentary evidence seems to

The Norman motte has found a new use.

point to its being a Norman moated mound similar to ones shown in the Bayeux tapestry. The mound would have been protected by a stockade, and a nearby stream probably supplied water for the moat. Following the stream to the south brings us to the Vineyard. This name takes us back to the times of the monks, when a vineyard would have been a part of an important estate such as that of Abingdon Abbey. The stream which has now disappeared, would have marked an appropriate boundary line and Stert Street, running in a straight line to the abbey gateway, very much gives the feel of an old boundary.

Stert Street is a mix of a street with modern office buildings next to medieval houses. There are some fine façades especially above first-floor level. Sadly, there is little sign of the first floors being used as dwellings and, in places, there are signs of neglect. On the left is a large yard containing the Railway public house. Such a name usually indicates a station. Predictably enough we find its remains. There is very little to see besides platforms and some track but enough to show the extent of the yard and the fact that this was a terminus. The lack of a through line would have prevented expansion in the railway age such as happened at Reading, Didcot and Swindon, and may explain the lack of Victorian building and the consequent drop in Abingdon's status, leading to Reading becoming the county town. This explains the mystery of a county police station in what is no longer a county town.

Returning to the Market Square, the route turns left through the arch to the abbey grounds and down Checker Walk to the remaining domestic buildings of the abbey. This area provides enough material for a separate investigation. So, passing the unusual lantern chimney, we go through the Slype to Thames Street, leaving that challenge for another time.

Thames Street itself provides clues to confirm that several earlier guesses were correct. First, the sound of rushing water and the name Abbey Mill confirm the presence of a water mill. Part of this is converted into the hotel and the water-wheel still turns in the restaurant.

Second, set in the accommodation bridge to the hotel car park are two black objects. This is Gasworks Bridge and the two objects are the ends of retorts, in which coal was heated to turn it into coke and release gas – the old town gas. This is the site of the old town gasworks, confirming our original impression that the area had been cleared for some industrial purpose. The coal was delivered by water.

The lantern chimney at Abingdon Abbey.

Third, under the bridge you can see a large hole disgorging water. In direct line with Stert Street and the stream by the Motte, this is the culverted River Stert. It was originally an open stream and did indeed mark the abbey boundary.

With the return to Bridge Street, our walk is complete. We have seen little sign of the wool trade, which brought about Abingdon's early prosperity, though the surviving cattle market indicates the town's importance as an agricultural centre. There is, however, more than enough to whet the appetite for further inquiry, and that alone makes the walk worthwhile.

Extramural Activities

WALK 12

Route: *Wapping, Mile End, Whitechapel, Spitalfields, Shad Thames, Rotherhithe (6 miles)*

Map: *Street atlas of London*

The walk starts outside Wapping Underground Station. Because of the complexity of this route, the walk is described in blocks, with directions at the beginning of each section.

Our first walk was in a remote, sparsely populated part of the country, and our final walk goes to the other extreme. The East End of London has always held a peculiar fascination. It is in the east end of a town or city that things happen: the east is the busy end. This is because the prevailing south-west wind keeps the air to the west clean, so creating an area of desirable residences.

The area we are to explore stands outside the city walls. Traditionally, the respectable burghers lived inside the city, the administrative centre, while the tradesmen were busy outside the back door. The basic element round which the town evolved is the river. The first settlement was at the river's crossing-point, and the walk begins at a present-day crossing-point – Wapping Underground Station, at the northern end of the Thames tunnel built by Marc Brunel.

The first view of the Thames: Wapping Underground Station to St Paul's Church in The Highway via Wapping Walk, Glamis Road and west down The Highway

Before continuing east along Wapping High Street what can we see of the Underground Station? There are lifts from the platforms and behind the fascia is the top of a large circular shaft. Keep it in mind for later. Emerging from the Underground station, our first impression is one of claustrophobia. Tall buildings line narrow streets. These are warehouses, but unlike the low warehouses we saw at Abingdon these have four or five storeys. However, like the

Abingdon warehouses, these are being converted into flats. As river traffic has declined, more and more of these warehouses have fallen empty. Gunn Wharf is a typical conversion. There are still signs of loading platforms, and cranes high on the side of the building. These were wharves for large commercial shipping and they line both banks of the river. There is no towpath or access along the river front, and access to the water is down little alleys leading to steps, each with a name. The one here is Wapping Dock Stairs. Street names play a special part in recalling the past: close by are Cinnamon, Penang and Chandler streets.

Not all the warehouses have been turned into residential accommodation. There are still signs of commercial use – a wine warehouse, a recording studio – while the road itself carries a constant stream of traffic. With a street this narrow the traffic must have been chaotic in its commercial heyday. The wear on the road surface is enormous, and here and there sets can be seen through the asphalt. In the road surface are a large number of cast-iron covers. These are for the services and each is marked appropriately: some G.P.O., others M.W.B. for Metropolitan Water Board, and one which may be less familiar, bearing the initials L.H.P.

Further along the warehouses are still being used. Goods are still raised by the old hand cranes, which are very well designed:

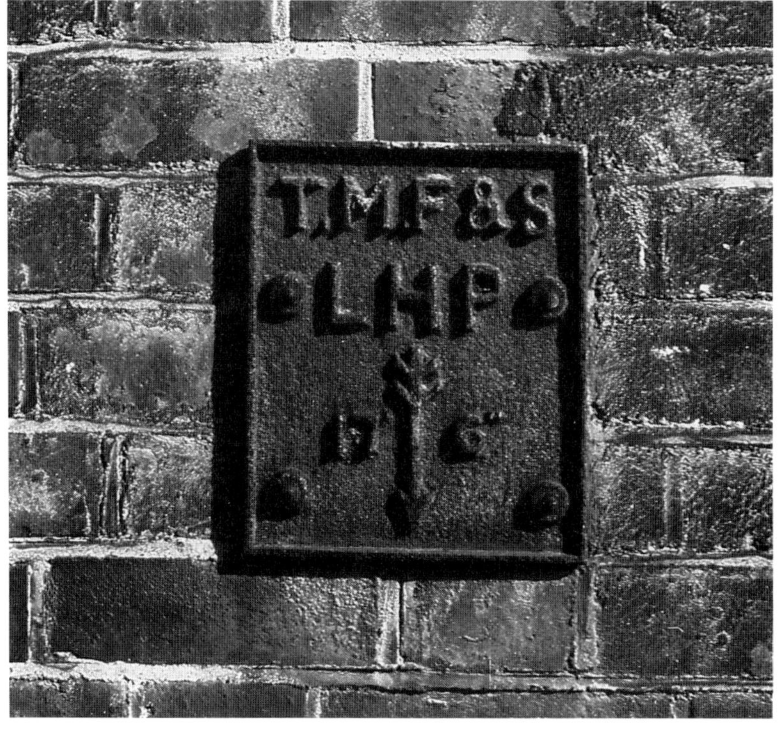

A London Hydraulic Plate on the wall at Goodman's Fields.

The changing face of the docks. Shadwell Dock, now unused, with a bridge that will never lift again, is overlooked by new housing and tower blocks.

mounted on pillars, they can swing through 180° and thus service two bays. The chains for controlling them run into the building through little windows and the control cab hangs on the side of the wall like a leech. On this stretch of the road three different designs of cannon are being used as bollards. Turning right into Wapping Wall there are more signs of cobbles and a trail of L.H.P. covers; and here, opposite the Prospect of Whitby pub, is a building bearing a plaque with the same initials. A high brick wall surrounds an industrial complex with a chimney, engine and boiler-houses. There is also a house fronting the road, probably for a manager. Despite the ivy, the plaque on the wall can be clearly seen to read 'London Hydraulic Company 1890'. In use until 1976, this was the last plant in London producing hydraulic power. The advantage of hydraulic power over other forms of energy is that energy can be stored and used as required. Water drawn from the Thames was filtered and stored in enormous cast-iron reservoirs before being pumped through 200 miles of underground pipes at a pressure of 800 pounds per square inch. Looking around the immediate area you can find many applications of this power. Round the corner in Shadwell dock the two lifting-bridges were hydraulically driven, as were many of the dockyard cranes and capstans. Besides these and other obvious examples, the power was harnessed to work lifts in Kensington, safety curtains in theatres and the cabaret floor at the Savoy.

Shadwell Basin gives a good side view of the London Hydraulic Company. Coal for the engine boilers was delivered here, craned in by hydraulic power, of course. At Shadwell the first signs of the docks' decline are evident. The old basin, marked by the lifting-bridges at either end, was part of a large complex of docks now being redeveloped. Some are being filled in, others adapted for other uses; this one for canoeists and other leisure activities. But signs of former use are still there, in chains along the banks

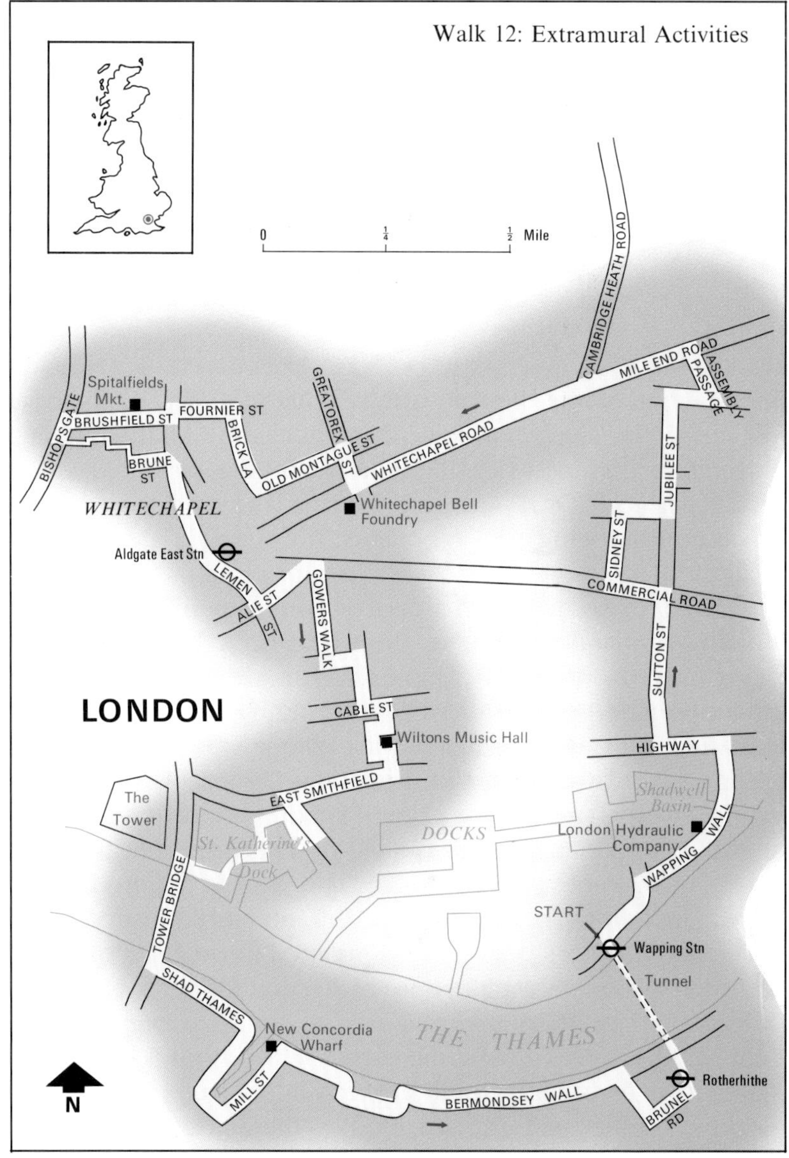

The London Hydraulic Company's Wapping factory has been designed to present a handsome face to the road.

and bollards that look as if they had been designed by Barbara Hepworth or Henry Moore. Sadly, the entrance from the Thames is permanently closed.

At The Highway the high dock walls date this as a nineteenth-century enclosed dock, a Victorian attempt to stop pilfering. Here too there are examples of three stages of council housing: first the Victorian flats, sombre and functional, each one having a balcony for fresh air; then the later high-rise version, still with balcony; and finally there is the modern small house development of brick and tile. These latter illustrate the theory of defensible space, and each individual garden is well looked after, which gives the area a distinctly suburban look. The communal piece of grass in front of the houses is untended.

Our attention is caught by a church. A good wrought-iron gate with modern lamps well in keeping leads to St Paul's churchyard. It is a little complex of its own with a church school and a rectory, demonstrating the important social role the church had in the area. On the rectory door a brass plate reads 'knock and ring', encouraging the use of an unusual Egyptian-looking door knocker. Inside, the church is most unusual. It was built in 1820 by an architect called Walters, and had a light, airy atmosphere. The roof has one large, shallow dome, and marbled wooden pillars support a simple balcony. The sense of space is created by high walls and ceiling built in long sweeping spans with no internal supports. We are told that the architect was also an engineer who had designed bridges. There are some interesting later art nouveau windows.

Glimpses of Victoriana: The Highway to Sidney Street via King David Street, Sutton Street and Commercial Road

This whole area has been drastically redeveloped for local authority housing and Cable Street, once notorious as a red light

Signs of immigration: this synagogue in Commercial Road shows it belongs in two cultures, carrying a date for both the Jewish and the Gregorian calendar.

district, has been tamed. However, there are odd signs of the old days. The Dover Castle pub has a characteristic green tiled front and the railway passes overhead on a long, arched viaduct. The spaces 'underneath the arches' are used as garages and stores, nowhere going to waste. The quiet of Sutton Street gives way to busy Commercial Road. This is a mix of a street, the first ingredient being a stone Star of David marking the synagogue of Jacob. The combination of being near the docks and in the cheaper end of the city has attracted successive waves of immigrants to this part of London including Huguenot refugees from France in the seventeenth century, Jews from eastern Europe and Germany earlier in the present century and, most recently, Bengalis. As it is a major thoroughfare there are also some grand houses, well proportioned but scaled down from London's finer terraces, an East End version of West End posh.

Rebellion and Restoration: Sidney Street to Mile End Road via Sidney Square, Jubilee Street, Redman's Road and Assembly Passage

At the corner of Sidney Street is a block of flats called Siege House. Here in 1911 the young Winston Churchill, then Home Secretary, directed the siege against Peter the Painter and his fellow anarchists. There is little now to show how the street once looked until Sidney Square is reached. This area is being revived as, with the decline in industry, the air becomes cleaner. Its increased desirability is illustrated by an epidemic of burglar alarm boxes. Careful restoration is making a derelict area come to life, and the details of windows, pillars and decorations are looking as new. The new houses are being built sympathetically, retaining the three-storey façade but, reflecting the times, using mass-produced materials such as windows without glazing bars. Along Jubilee Street and Redman's Road the three storeys reduce to two. It is fun trying to recognize the original features of the neighbourhood. Which building was a shop? Which window has the original glazing bars? Did the Gothic style of window come earlier or later than the square sashes? A funeral director's sports a carving of a muse, or at least a well built young lady. Juniper Street (now the entrance to a housing estate) harks back to the Wapping spice street names. On the other hand, there could be another interpretation as, in nearby Redman's Road, there is an industrial building with chimney, loading bays and very secure doors with bars. It was the Mile End Distillery and bonded warehouse. Juniper flavours gin.

The cobbled Assembly Passage leading to Mile End Road is still a

The style of the ship reflects the date of the building: a detail on the parapet of the Trinity House almshouses.

The Trinity House almshouses.

busy alley. On one side is a packaging company, using machinery driven by overhead belts; and on the right the nose detects a smokehouse, whose smoked foods can be bought in the adjoining shop.

The Main Thoroughfare: Mile End Road and Whitechapel Road

The entry to the main road is under an old arch. Immediately opposite is a large 1920s shopping emporium in a vaguely art deco style. Turn left, past the old house supporting the arch from Assembly Passage and a grander house which is now the rent office. The road is wide and appears even wider as another small road runs parallel to it, separated by a pavement. Both roads are fronted by substantial buildings, and may at one time have been separated by a row of houses, now demolished. One building on the other side has been established since 1695. It is a group of almshouses built to house '28 decayed masters and commanders of ships or ye widows of such'. The grounds were given by Captain Henry Mudd and they are maintained by the Corporation of Trinity House. Next to it is a much later and rather grand municipal building with wide doors and special access to the main road. It is marked 'L.C.C.', and its position and proportions suggest a former fire station.

Crossing the Cambridge Heath Road you reach the first of many good Victorian pubs. The one with a converted exterior gas lamp is called the Blind Beggar. It must be the brewery tap, as next to it the old Mann's brewery is still in use. Other pubs are large with imposing façades, a reminder that this was an area of music halls; even in the side streets some frontages show signs of Victorian grandeur to attract the public.

Mile End Road has now become Whitechapel Road; opposite a street market is the London Hospital. Despite the grandeur of the main block, this is a mass of buildings incorporating a variety of styles, from pedimented entrance through Victorian wards with enclosed iron bridges to modern portakabins. It also takes up an incredibly large area, encompassing whole streets and, in one part, a pretty square. Next comes an indication of a new immigrant

A modern planned development off Brick Lane contrasts with the surrounding area.

population: the gold crescent surmounting a large dome and minarets marks the new London Mosque. Beyond is a group of much older buildings at the side of Fieldgate Street. It was here in 1738 that Thomas Lester moved the Whitechapel Bell Foundry from Aldgate. Bells are still cast at the foundry, which made both Big Ben and the Liberty Bell. The workshops, with a well blended modern extension, have a fine shop front onto Whitechapel Road.

The Immigrant Weavers: Whitechapel Road to Spitalfields Market via Greatorex Street, Old Montague Street, Brick Lane and Fournier Street

On the corner of Old Montague Street is an industrial complex of a type we have not seen since Skipton – a single-storey workshop with northern lights. Farther on we meet more signs of the textile industry. In Brick Lane there is a modern housing development, a 1980s rethink reverting to catslide roofs and uneven angles. This is serviced by a very well designed health centre, full of columns and light. Down Fashion Street is the Moorish Bazaar. Built as a Jewish market, it failed and was turned into a textile mill. Jewish culture has given way to the Asian community, whose presence is reflected in the local primary school advertising its open day in English and Bengali.

At Fournier Street the area takes on a different dimension. Here is a complete eighteenth-century street of grand houses. The details are superb. There are porches with decorated columns and carved doorcases, embossed drainpipes, shutters, stone keystones to the windows and decorative plasterwork. In the top storey of the buildings there are rows of windows in wooden frames added after the main structures were built. We have seen top-floor lights before in Yorkshire where there were weavers. These clues, together with later research, show that these houses were inhabited by Huguenot silk weavers. They bought them cheaply as this was a speculative development outside the city wall. Conversion into workshops led to the area's debasement. From that time most of the houses – with their superbly panelled and staircased interiors which can be glimpsed through an open door – have been used for textile manufacture. It is worth making a diversion to Wilkes Street to see more. Christ Church was built by Hawksmoor, altered by many, and is now a theatre. The high baroque interior is worth a look.

Across the road in Brushfield Street is Spitalfields Market, built in traditional style with iron columns supporting a pitched roof – a pleasing functional building. Opposite is the Fruit and Wool Exchange, a curious combination.

Eighteenth-century houses in Fournier Street, the elegant façade topped by weavers' windows.

Commerce and Leisure: Spitalfields to Tower Bridge via Bishopsgate, Sands Row, Artillery Passage, Brune Street, Leman Street, Alie Street, Hooper Street, Grace's Alley, Thomas More Street and St Katharine's Dock

At Bishopsgate we enter the City of London and turn left down Royal Artillery Row. The area is a splendid pocket of eighteenth-century shops with shutters, warehouses and narrow alleys. However, the names have a distinctly lethal ring – first, the Gun pub, then all this mention of artillery, and now a pub called the Grape Shot. Later investigation showed that this was an area of military training grounds. In Brune Street a delicatessen, an importer established in 1877 and two warehouses with cast-iron fittings and a crane border a building erected in 1902 which was a 'soup kitchen for the Jewish poor'.

From here we turn south through streets busy with markets and, through a muddling system of pedestrian underpasses, cross over to Leman Street. In Alie Street a German Lutheran church gives a clue to another group of immigrants. The area round Hooper Street is full of warehouses. There are the usual cranes but with pipework – once more the sign of hydraulic power. In the road are cobbles and railway lines. This is strange as there are viaducts above supporting a main line and various sidings leading towards us. There is also an accumulator tower, so there must have been a large amount of machinery driven by hydraulic power. In fact this whole area was the goods terminus of the London, Tilbury and Southend Railway Company. It was on two levels, trucks being raised and lowered in lifts, and a hydraulic capstan was still to be seen until recently. Now the few remaining sheds are being redeveloped.

Passing under the viaduct, it is worth noting the differences in style and materials of the new section being built. Looking down from Grace's Alley you can see the rear of the only remaining building in the centre of the square. It is large, with a semicircular end, an iron staircase and blank sides with no windows. There is a small lantern on the top reminiscent of the smoke outlet of a theatre. The front of the building has a portico, and the word 'Wiltons' is carved above the entrance. In 1858 it was announced that 'Mr Wilton having found his old music room totally inadequate to accommodate his great influx of visitors has been compelled to erect a hall on a more extended scale'. Old photographs of the interior show an ornate balcony supported by corkscrew columns. The building is currently being worked on and we can only look forward to its opening.

An attempt has been made to preserve St Katharine's Dock, London's oldest enclosed dock, by refurbishing the warehouses and by introducing a maritime museum. It is very difficult to detect anything in this area. True, there are some large cast-iron columns but these could have come from anywhere. The main warehouse block has been so altered that it gives no clue to its original use. There are occasional glimpses of architectural detail, for example vaulted brick arches springing off iron beams and supporting brick floors, a form of fireproof flooring developed in the cotton industry. The way to treat the area is to enjoy what you can. The various accommodation bridges over the marina are fun and on the day we went, besides the permanent set-pieces, there was a good range of boats to see, including a fine steam-powered launch and two Thames sailing barges. There are still examples of dock paraphernalia, such as the splendid bollards by the much-used lock. From here steps lead up past the new hotel to Tower Bridge. It is now possible to cross the bridge using the upper gallery. This is well worth doing, not only for the views up and down river, but to see how the bridge was constructed, the full story of which is told in a museum in the engine-houses on the south side of the river. The bridge was connected to the London hydraulic system, but this was only for emergencies as it had two steam engines of its own.

The claustrophobic effect of warehouses at Shad Thames.

Return to the Docks: Tower Bridge to Rotherhithe via Shad Thames, Mill Street and Bermondsey Wall

From Tower Bridge to Greenwich the south bank of the Thames was once lined with one dock after another. Only one is left, many have been filled in, and some were built over as more and more warehousing was needed. In turn, these large buildings have now become derelict and are being converted into flats. The first group of buildings is Butler Wharf. Inside are columns and brick arches. In the centre is the main wharf entrance, with gate columns and round windows for a bit of prestige. On the walls cranes and iron cleats abound, and the buildings are linked by overhead bridges. An incongruous note is struck by a disused corner shop. Painted on the brick you can just discern the words 'Toilet goods, Patent medicines and prescriptions'.

Passing Maguire Street we were hit by the smell of turmeric. Still working amongst this dereliction is a spice-grinding mill. Think what the aroma must have been like in the heyday of the docks! Shad Thames then turns abruptly inland. At the end of the road opposite are the Dock Head Stores, for here is the head of St Saviour's Dock. In the dock there are larger cranes and lighters, the latter sitting on the mud at low tide. In Mill Street we are back to large wharves, in this case New Concordia Wharf. New it looks in its modern conversion, but amongst the offices and flats there are still signs of an engine-house, a chimney and a water tower. As we continue more clues to the past appear. Jacob Street invokes the now disappeared Jacob's Island, mentioned in Oliver Twist, and the remains of 'St Saviour's Ironworks, Engineers and Smiths' echo the name of the old dock. Southwark cathedral was formerly known as St Saviour's parish church, indicating that this section of riverside was part of Southwark.

Bermondsey Wall leads us to Cherry Garden Pier, once used by Pepys. A lone warehouse in a desolate stretch of demolition is dated 1934, a sign that the area was still expanding between the wars. Across the river from the Royal Humane Society's life-saving apparatus, the river police station can be seen and, just past it, Gunn Wharf, where our walk started.

By the Ship public house our route takes us through a new estate to reach Rotherhithe. From Tower Bridge we have followed the commercial waterfront – a narrow band of development along the Thames. At Rotherhithe this broadens into a waterside town with church, houses and pub strangely reminiscent of Faversham.

Village and Tunnel: Rotherhithe to Wapping via Mayflower Street, St Mary's Church Street, Brunel Road and Rotherhithe Underground Station

The first building we reach in Rotherhithe village is the Mayflower pub, whose name reminds us that it was from here that the famous ship left before going to America via Plymouth. The church also has echoes of the sea. A plaque on the wall is to Captain Anthony Wood, who died in 1625. This must have come from an earlier church as the present one is an early Georgian building. Rotherhithe Picture Research Library is situated in an eighteenth-century timber-framed warehouse. Looking at the timber supports to the upper floor you can see a good example of 'knees', the 90° bracket of a ship's hull – a sensible re-use of materials. At the side of the churchyard is a small building like a sentry box, marked Watch House. Not a dry spot for the local constable but a lodge for an attendant watching for body snatchers. A little further on there is a squat brick building, which, to judge by its construction and doors, was used for industrial purposes. Close by is a circular brick wall of similar dimensions to that at Wapping Underground Station. A board explains that these were the engine-house and shaft used by the Brunels to build the first tunnel under the Thames, started in 1825 and opened to the public in 1843. It now carries the tube line from Rotherhithe Station, in the appropriately named Brunel Road, to Wapping, where the ends of the tunnels, with their characteristic horseshoe shape, are clearly visible. The lift shaft, which we saw from the outside at the start of the walk, is the original entrance shaft built in 1840.

Possibly because we have kept to the river for a lot of the walk, we have seen virtually nothing of old London. With land at a premium, all early sites have been built on. However, John Stow's *Survey of London*, of 1603, throws some fascinating sidelights on the area. He notes that Wapping was an execution place for hanging pirates, 'but since the gallows being often removed farther off, a continual street or filthy strait passage, with alleys of small tenements'. He also mentions 'a large highway, with fair elm trees on both sides' – a description that might fit Mile End Road. But to match up his descriptions with a modern plan of London is properly a winter task for the armchair detective.

FOLLOWING UP LEADS

So far we have set great store by observation, but you cannot always solve a problem just by looking. So in this part of the book we shall be suggesting how the landscape detective can find out more about what he has seen or is about to see.

Walking the Beat

All our walks have been just that: the landscape detective is no use in a car. A bicycle is better, but everything passes so fast that there is no time to digest information and it is difficult to stop and examine things. For example, Claverton pumping station is on the banks of the River Avon. It is a water-powered pump which carries water up to the Kennet and Avon Canal above. Cycling along not far from the site, all the clues were noted: a building in the valley, on the River Avon, what looked like an outlet into the canal, a piece of piping lying along the towpath. But it was only on checking the map a quarter of a mile further on that this detective realized he had passed the pump and had to go back.

So it is by slowly putting the pieces together that a picture builds. It was impressed on us time and time again how much there is to be found which is not obvious. In the Forest of Dean, for example, we followed an old railway track. Not content with that, we looked for more clues. There was nothing in the track bed, no sleepers used as fencing, nor any other clue. However, at one point beside the track there was a stone wall. On looking closely at the stones we found some stone sleeper blocks, indicating that this was once a tramway. This could have been discovered by later research, but there was so much more satisfaction in finding the extra clue on the ground and using the map only for verification. If we had been content simply to call this an old railway before hurrying on we would have missed it. There is also great delight when on a fifth or sixth visit you find something new when you thought you already knew an area well. In our case it was the main gunpowder complex at Oare. We knew the waterway and the magazine, but it was only as a result of approaching the site from a completely new angle that we found the complex at the end of the canal.

Reading the Map

The book started with maps and all the way through we rely heavily on them. For all the walks in the country we used the Ordnance Survey 1:50,000 series. That means that the scale is about 1¼ inches to the mile. For detailed work in towns we also used local street plans. The first essential is to be able to read a grid reference. This is the six-figure number that marks a position on an Ordnance Survey map. To take an example: suppose that you have sheet 164 of the 1:50 000 Ordnance Survey series (the Oxford area) and you are given the reference 499969. The first three digits are the eastings, and the first two refer to the numbers at the top and bottom of the sheet labelling the vertical lines – 49 tells you to look between lines 49 and 50. The third digit refers to imaginary tenths of that distance, so 499 is 9/10 of the way along the line. Similarly 969, the northings, tells you to look for a point 9/10 of the way from 96 to 97 in the horizontal lines. The intersection of these two lines is the reference point, in this case Abingdon Bridge. To give a map reference, simply reverse the process. With a six-figure reference it is possible to pinpoint a location to within 100 metres. Sometimes four-figure references are given to designate the 1-kilometre square marked by two grid lines. Occasionally two letters precede a reference. They serve to make the reference unique – the numbers recur at 100-kilometre intervals.

Locating a site on the map is one thing, but using the map to find where you are on the ground is quite a different problem. Often, if you are following a path, you need to do no more than check the curves and turnings shown on the map. Another useful check can be made from the levels on the ground: the brown contour lines show the lie of the land and the closer they are together the more steeply the land slopes. It is often also a simple matter to check your actual position by looking for features on the map – such as a church, a wood, or a farm – which stand either side of your track and ahead of you. When you reach the point where an imaginary line drawn between the features crosses your track, then you have pinpointed your position.

It is even more important to know which way you are travelling, which is no problem if you find north. This can always be done if the sun is shining and you know the approximate time. At midday the sun is due south: at other times point the hour hand of the watch at the sun – the north-south line runs at the bisection of the hour hand and twelve o'clock. Do remember that this only works for Greenwich Mean Time. This sort of elementary map reading is of little help in really rough country. There you need a decent compass and the ability to take compass bearings. Those who plan walks in wild mountainous country should read one of the many books on the subject, and practise their map reading before setting off.

Visits and Guides

In writing the walks we have shown how an accumulation of clues builds up a picture. We have not tried to describe features that can be found outside our particular frame, even if they are well-known points of interest. However, a great deal of information can be enjoyably gained from visiting nearby churches, stately homes, or museums. Museums run by the county are particularly relevant as they concentrate on the local area and the appropriate records and archives. There are also a large number of private museums, often concerned with transport or buildings. We have mentioned the museum at Cotehele Quay in the Tamar Valley and the George Leatt Industrial and Folk Museum at Skipton. They represent two extremes. The first sets out to explain logically the characteristics of the immediate area; the other is more a collection of objects. It is hard to define these 'objects' in words – junk, ephemera, *objets d'art* – but all of them are fun. Here are knife sharpeners, bird scarers with clockwork timers, every kind of agricultural clutter, fork and rake; there are threshing machines, elevators, beet cutters – all collected and looked after by individuals who love to talk about them.

The pumping station at Westonzoyland is another private venture. We arranged to be there on a 'steaming day', when the engine was working. Most places like this have working days at varying intervals, and then there is something of a carnival atmosphere. This is when the hard work of restoration comes to fruition, and, there are often other things to see besides the main event. It is a time when enthusiasts gather and their enthusiasm infects everyone. It is also a useful time to collect local information.

Most buildings open to the public have their own guidebooks.

Some enlightened places have notices explaining what's what and what's where, though time after time we have been frustrated on heading for a board only to find that its purpose is not to inform but to instruct, by stating the by-laws or using a large number of sentences starting with the word 'Don't'.

Looking at Details

In order to work out the history of a building, the architect detective has to look at it in detail. *On the Dating of English Houses*, by J. T. Smith and E. M. Yates, shows very clearly how to look at an old building systematically. However, as with so many books, the examples it gives are nationally known buildings and usually true to their period.

The sort of problem facing the architect detective is that more often than not the house in question is not a perfect example. And, although dating is useful, what we are looking for is the evolution of a building – which might involve changing use as well as changing shape. With this in mind let us take a close look at three buildings, keeping to the Oxford Ordnance Survey map, sheet 164. Two are in Abingdon and one just outside the town.

From the outside, 17 West St Helen Street looks like a seventeenth-century shop. The front is plain rendered with symmetrical windows on the first and second floors and a large shop window on the ground floor. The entrance to the shop is through a door on the left under what could be a porch. It is this which should attract the detective's attention. The door is wide and has an arched top. Unusually, the sides of the door frame are large pieces of oak. To the left, at first-floor plate level, is a corbel to support a jetty, or overhang. This immediately puts back the date. The large shop window has been built out towards the pavement and the door marks the original ground-floor line. Inside, details of the timber frame are clearly visible, as is the original side wall of the building. In fact it is a classic late medieval building, whose later additions and adaptations conceal the original age of the building from the casual observer.

In East St Helen Street there is a building we noticed on the Abingdon walk. It is a small Georgian-fronted building next to a two-bay cottage – numbers 27a and 29. Seen from across the road, these two buildings display various odd features. Number 27a, the one on the right, has a brick front with a charming door and big sash windows. At the top there is a parapet ending in a decorated

The doorway of number 17, showing timber frame and overhanging support.

stone filial. The first-floor string course is in line with that of the house on the right, but the windows are in line with the cottages on the left. The steep, pitched roof, despite one part being retiled in modern tiles, is all of one structure with the house on the left, and there are symmetrically spaced dormer windows above both houses. What has happened is that at some point the right-hand bay of a three-bay Tudor building has been acquired and given a face-lift, to make it look more prosperous. It has been done without altering the roof line or adding an extra storey to enlarge the room with the gable on the second floor. It is in other words a purely cosmetic change. There has been change to the left-hand cottage. Larger windows have been put in and the sill beam, which is the lowest horizontal beam, has been refaced with York slab, an indication of a timber frame that almost certainly runs through both houses. Thus these two houses were once a single Tudor unit and both have been dressed up to look Georgian, one with the minimum and one with the maximum of effort.

We were driving west to Cothill when (at grid reference 467996) our attention was caught by a glimpse of water through a gap in the hedge and immediately following this a building with a wooden hoist cover overhanging the road. We stopped to investigate and heard the noise of a stream to the east. This made us wonder whether the building had once been a water mill. If so, the water we heard at a low level must have been its tail-race. Past the mill to the west there is a bump across the road and to the north leading from it a grass area which could once have been a millpond. Projected back to the building, the water would have met the mill at what now serves as a garage. The wall fronting the road has an over-large window with a substantial sill at about waggon height.

27a and 29 East St Helen Street: two houses that were originally one.

This must have been the main mill floor. Adjoining the mill is a prosperous house. The mill shows every sign of being a Victorian building with stone courses ending in brick quoins and windows with upright brick headers. The house is considerably earlier, suggesting that this was a replacement for an earlier mill building, probably timber-framed. Just to the east of the tail-race is another fine building. We thought that possibly this could have been another mill but the map marks a quarry, suggesting a possible alternative. At this point in our deliberations the owner of the house returned and told us that the mill was working until 1927,

The mill at Cothill.

the wheel being removed later to provide material for the Second World War.

Searching for Clues

At the end of a walk, instead of enjoying a sense of satisfaction, the mind is usually awash with unanswered questions, and where the landscape detective finishes the armchair detective takes over. Where did the dismantled railway run to and when was it closed? There are processes to investigate: how did a lime kiln operate? There are places to visualize: how did the Queen's Hotel look before the shopping precinct was built?

OLD MAPS

The first things to look for are large-scale maps. This is the quickest way of finding out what was where. Maps will only give you confirmation of what exists today, but that is a start. If what you want is not there the next thing to turn to is older maps. The oldest map we looked at was a map of Abingdon made in 1560. Besides showing the overall size of the town, it also told us how much of the old town remains. We were also able to compare the course of the Thames with its present-day line. The map shows a lock close to the bridge in the southernmost channel, the channel that is still the navigational route. What is such fun on these early maps is that any prominent feature is shown pictorially, not diagrammatically, so there is a splendid drawing of St Helen's Church with a cock weathervane as there is now, to a scale which, if accurate, would have collapsed the tower years ago.

Another map that we used was a reproduction of 'Crutchley's New Plan of London improved to 1829'. Comparing this with a modern street map it is easy to see what has survived. There was, of course, no Tower Bridge, but the Brunel tunnel is marked as 'projected'. (Privately printed maps such as these can be notoriously inaccurate, and proposed schemes were often included on a map after they had been abandoned.) There is a 'Jews Burial Ground' marked, and a workhouse in Whitechapel Road. Trinity Alms-Houses are marked, as are several others. The railway has not arrived but the docks and canals are well established. Mile End Road is shown as a wide thoroughfare, as wide as it is now, showing that nothing has been demolished to make the road wider since 1829 and probably not before, thus answering a question posed on our walk. Many of the streets have had their names changed or have disappeared, such as Vinegar Street and

Anchor and Hope Street. South of the river, the map shows ribbon development along the Thames, echoing the feeling we had in the London walk. Close to the water there are a lot of rope walks. These were long, straight, narrow stretches of land used for walking the ropes out as the yarn was twisted. Also marked is a much more compact industrial site for manufacturing iron cable, showing progression as iron replaces rope. The end of St Saviour's Dock is marked Dockhead, hence the Dockhead Stores we spotted on the walk. There is even a fishpond on the map but no trace of this remains. Some of the roads have the same shapes as they do now but slightly different names: thus Marygood Street has become Marigold Street. There are millponds, factories for glue and soap, exotic names like Lemon Valley, and the Grand Surrey Canal.

The first accurate maps were the Ordnance Survey maps. First produced for defence purposes in 1790, the original Ordnance Survey maps of Kent, Surrey and Sussex were gradually extended to the whole country. The second series is the most useful, as the turn of the nineteenth century saw a 6 inch to the mile map and also a 25 inch to the mile version. It was this larger scale that helped to unveil the mystery of Skipton station, among other things. As this was a time of great expansion the second series shows the original state of much of what we see today. It was intriguing to find Abingdon's long-demolished workhouse and to trace the course of Faversham's railway lines. These two examples show how it is possible to compare features seen today with those shown on early maps. To build up a complete picture, you need to look at a series of maps of different dates, so that the whole process of evolution can be followed.

Mention ought to be made of specialist maps. For example, we have found invaluable a railway gazetteer which shows every line and station in the country, including now disused lines and dates of closure. There are specialist Ordnance Survey maps such as those of Hadrian's Wall and Roman Britain. And, although geological maps can be difficult to decipher, the effort is often well worth making.

BOOKS AND DOCUMENTS

There are two sorts of reference works: primary and secondary sources. Primary sources give the information directly; secondary sources give someone else's account of that information. A copy of the Act of Parliament for the construction of the Grand Junction Canal would be a primary source: an account of it in the history of the canal a secondary. Primary sources come in a tremendous variety of forms. There are minutes of council meetings, census returns (though material less than a hundred years old is not available as it contains personal details), street directories, trade directories and many more. All these provide a lot of background for walks.

Old town guides, for example, often contain advertisements from which you can check on the firms and businesses of the area. The guidebook to Abingdon for 1937 showed the old gaol as having badminton courts and informed the visitor that 'the Abbey Buildings can be viewed on application to Sergeant at Mace, No. 2 The Abbey'. Number 2 The Abbey no longer exists but could have been one of the cottages where all that is left today is a brick floor. It is easily seen below the lantern chimney mentioned on page 179. The book is also useful as a guide to the social life of the town. Lists of societies and descriptions of the town's regalia and customs all help to complete the picture.

From guides to histories: most areas have books written about them with a varying degree of success. Some, especially those written in the Victorian era, can be very dry. Sometimes the only factual information comes in the form of financial accounts, which may be important but are rarely interesting. One can, however, find descriptions of individual buildings and compare their condition then with their present state.

One invaluable source of help for the architect detective is Pevsner's series on the *Buildings of England*. For the principal towns he starts with the churches, moves on to municipal buildings and ends with a perambulation, in which there is a brief description of the other main buildings. The buildings are explained succinctly, with a large number of technical terms. However, each volume contains a fully illustrated glossary so there is no need to be discouraged by too many unknown words. It is surprising how quickly these terms are learned, not by rote but by use. The disadvantage of Pevsner is that he limits himself to buildings of architectural worth, and there are many buildings that are of great interest to the historian though they have no architectural merit at all.

Another much-used reference series is the *Victoria History of the Counties of England*. This is an enormous work, still being written, and some counties are better documented than others. Earlier volumes tend to concentrate on antiquarian and ecclesiastical history, but the later editions include rather more social and economic history. In general, the later the edition the more help it is. This is the work we often turn to first, stifling a groan if the relevant volume was printed before the 1920s. It is worth remembering that both Pevsner and the *Victoria County History* use the old county boundaries; the latter also uses the even older subdivisions of hundreds. Thus Abingdon comes under Berkshire, and Skipton under the Hundred of Craven. Finding your way around takes a little practice.

It is not enough simply to find a book on your chosen subject area, for not all books are reliable. The most valuable are those with good bibliographies and references. One must necessarily take a certain amount on trust, and there is no real substitute for research with primary sources. But, even if you have neither the time nor the inclination to go back to primary sources, it is a great comfort to find that the author can quote them. Otherwise you have no means of telling whether a 'fact' you are reading is fully documented or simply based on hearsay and rumour. One of the authors once made a joking reference to a building and was startled to find that his joke was taken seriously and duly appeared in print in someone else's book. Often information needs to be collected from a number of books before the complete picture emerges, and a good bibliography will help by leading you to different sources.

NEWSPAPERS AND MAGAZINES

Here is another good source of information. Newspapers and magazines give an event an immediacy often lacking in official sources. In a report of the railway smash at Abingdon in 1908, the local paper tells that 'some pigs in a van close to the engine did not appear to have been disturbed, being found apparently asleep'. Scanning the 'hundred years ago' section in a local paper can often turn up another little piece of information to complete the jigsaw, but it was in a current events section that we saw an item linked to the gunpowder industry in Faversham. A tin of gunpowder had been found in one of the huts on the allotments. It had been there for many years and was only found on the death of the elderly tenant.

Hunting for information in newspapers is not easy. A few are indexed but it is best to approach the subject by date, allowing an appropriate margin. A good story will be followed up in future editions, so it is best to do a thorough search.

PICTORIAL SOURCES

If we had not come across the painting of the Abingdon waterfront we would have missed a chunk of detecting. Pictures, however, are not always reliable, being painted with a certain amount of artistic licence and style. The old Abingdon map recorded a 'flash' lock. It is difficult to describe in words how such a lock actually worked, but a print of a Thames flash lock discovered hanging on a sitting-room wall made all clear.

Another useful source of information is old photographs. We were lucky to find the old photograph of the Abingdon wharf, which gave us the clue to the area's commercial transport system. Many pubs now have these old photographs as decoration. At least the photographs are an accurate representation of the past, unlike many of the illustrations found on inn signs.

Collections of old photographs have been published for many areas. Again using Abingdon as an example, M. J. Thomas's book *Abingdon in Camera* provided an answer to many queries. One in particular puzzled us for some time. Standing under the county hall, we were intrigued by the hotchpotch of municipal buildings to the right of the abbey gateway. There is evidence of modern stone building, with steps leading from the corner of Bridge Street to first-floor level. As this is the most prominent feature, it distracts the eye from a porticoed house round the corner. A photograph of 1890 shows quite a different aspect. There is a shop called the Coffee Tavern on the corner, now demolished and replaced by the steps, and behind this is an ornamental gateway with plaque and figures leading to Roysse's School, later Abingdon School. The gateway, the plaque and the figures are still there, but the gate itself has been replaced by a door and the decorated top has been incorporated in the new steps to form the balustrade. So there is nothing you can see to tell you that this door was once a gate leading into a yard surrounded by buildings. But, by looking at what is left behind, the old pattern begins to make sense. Using the old gate as a fixed point, the open square behind must be Roysse's yard. Along one side is the old school building, still called Roysse's Room, and the frontage of the adjacent house, now the local authority's legal department, shows the signs of arching over the windows which can be seen in an 1865 school photograph. This was a particularly satisfying piece of detection as I have passed this part of Abingdon many times and thought, 'There is the Roysse room, part of the old grammar school and the town's heritage.' However, it was not until we bothered to look closely and find out precisely what was what that the whole complex of the school made sense.

ORAL SOURCES

One of the great pleasures of being a landscape detective is that

The Abingdon School photographs give the clue to later development. The house with the white rendered wall has been demolished, so the square is no more, as can be seen in the contemporary view. (The older photograph is reproduced by kind permission of the Headmaster of Abingdon School).

people talk to you. When we were exploring the Uplees terminus of the Davington Light Railway, a friendly person came out of her house and explained that it used to be the office where workers were searched for matches before going into the gunpowder factories. Often a simple inquiry will elicit a flood of information, though some answers must be treated with a little scepticism. We were told by a local at Newbold that the remains of the old canal tunnel were in fact an air-raid shelter constructed in 1942; this 'fact' was supported by the ultimate proof – 'I remember it being built'. Another pleasure is talking to craftsmen, though one should be wary not to distract them from their work. Like people who live in old buildings, craftsmen take a pride in what they know and often like to share their knowledge with others. There are also strange things to discover. At St Oswald's Cross near Wall we talked to a doctor who was collecting soil samples from known early battle sites to send to America for bacteriological research.

Locating Material

The starting-point is the public library. Most have a certain amount of material on their local area, and you will often find a librarian with knowledge prompted by personal interest in the subject. Larger libraries have specific local history sections staffed by specialists. We all start by asking rather tentatively, but meet such enthusiasm that it becomes a pleasure to seek help. The local section will contain far more than just books; there may be all kinds of material, from newspapers to photographs. The local history section of Tower Hamlets library had a wealth of material on Wilton's Music Hall – newspaper cuttings, programmes, brochures, and a set of photographs of the interior taken by the local camera club. Information gained in local libraries can lead to other sources. Investigating the London Hydraulic Factory we relied on a general book about hydraulics until we were referred to the magazine published by the Greater London Industrial Archaeology Society (GLIAS). That suggests another source. Any public library carries a list of local societies. The county archaeology and historical societies usually publish regular magazines, many of which go back several decades. Many publish occasional indexes, and a diverting afternoon can be had looking at these. Some have a subject index covering not just the society's own publications but a wider range of books, articles and periodicals. Many places now have community societies and other local groups such as industrial archaeology societies. They too provide a fund of information, publish magazines and hold regular meetings, and some have photographic archives and tape recordings. One that immediately comes to mind is a recording made by a society of an old lady who lived by the Thames and Medway Canal recalling its working days.

Many documents are housed in the county record offices. These contain a wide variety of national, ecclesiastical and local county reports. There are property deeds, details of quarter sessions and school records. The information there can be used to trace places and people, industry and transport. County record offices are not places to go for a general browse and several of them insist on your booking time to work there.

Research material is not always available locally and even if it is it may not be convenient to go to that locality. If you find you have a query about a walk in Northumberland after you have got back home to Abingdon it may not be much help to be told to go back up to Northumberland again. So there may often be a case for using the national records. The principal repository of documents is the Public Record Office at Kew, though as with the county offices it is essential to know what you are looking for before you arrive. There are no shelves here for browsers – documents are ordered up through a computerized system. The great repository of newspapers is the British Museum Newspaper Library, at Colindale, London. Sometimes you may find a reference to an old and rare book which you will have to locate at one of the major libraries. The most important of these is the British Library at the British Museum, which you can use by obtaining a temporary ticket, provided you can convince the authorities that you have a genuine need to go there. The thing to remember is that information is usually available somewhere if you delve deep enough.

Bringing the Past to Life

All this talk of record offices and source material may sound unduly academic. In fact the greatest pleasure for landscape detectives often comes from incidental distractions. Like Autolycus in *The Winter's Tale*, we are 'snappers up of unconsidered trifles'.

While history at school may seem boring, exploration on the ground can stimulate a desire for more historical background. Having walked close to Sedgemoor and seen the lock on the door of Westonzoyland church where prisoners were held afterwards, we went straight to an account of the battle, the last to be fought on English soil. In 1685 the Duke of Monmouth with three thousand men failed to defeat the King's army of about the same number because of their inability to cross a wide drain, the Bussex Rhine. The battle was followed by fearful retribution, led by Judge Jeffreys and meted out at the 'Bloody Assizes'. As so often happens, there is a coincidental link with another walk – the judge ended his career by being beheaded at the Tower, having been seized disguised as a sailor at Wapping. Looking across Sedgemoor's almost unchanged landscape at dusk, with its still, quiet atmosphere, it is possible to imagine the battle quite easily, a feeling not unlike that which we felt at the pele tower at Chollerford. Incidentally, it is worth visiting places at different times of the day and in different seasons. The difference is quite dramatic and can be very evocative.

On a more mundane level it can be enjoyable to read both contemporary and later reports of the construction of artefacts seen on the walks. One of the most interesting is the account of the building of the Thames Tunnel by Brunel father and son, particularly the quotations from the Brunel diaries and the account of the second flooding of the tunnel on 12 January 1828, when Isambard saved the lives of several workmen and was himself injured.

History and geography are usually linked. Having followed Hadrian's Wall across the country, we wanted to find out how the wall was supplied from the south. It was a surprise to find that in Roman times Scotch Corner was as important a junction as it is today. Modern road builders often find that their predecessors have surveyed the easiest route. On a smaller scale, we learned that a military road was built on Hadrian's Wall in 1745 as part of the campaign to suppress the Scottish uprising – the road we walked at St Oswald's Cross.

Will Kemp, the Shakespearian clown, came into our conversation while we were walking in London. On 10 February 1600 he wagered that he would dance from London to Norwich. 'He set forward from the Lord Mayor's towards the Lord of Norwich through Whitechapel, Mile End and Stratford Bow.' The account suggests that this must have been the main route out of the city, as, having wagered, he would want to pass as many people as possible. Contemporary reports of this 'nine days' wonder' make it possible to trace his route through Romford and Bury St Edmunds. So far we have confined ourselves to the non-fiction section of libraries. However, there is much to be gained from fiction also. Obviously a well researched historical novel can give substantial background to a period or place, but there are less substantial references, just as much fun, which can add small pieces to the jigsaw.

There are two lengthy works directly connected with the walks in this book. The first is Wordsworth's epic poem *The White Doe of Rylestone*. This recounts the legend of the dispute between the Nortons and the Cliffords, with many a reference to Norton Tower on the moors above Skipton. The other is an earlier piece and concerns the murder of Thomas Arden, Mayor of Faversham. One might well ask what information can be gleaned from an Elizabethan play, but there is material there, albeit not immediately obvious. Not only are the various settings of the plot of interest, there are also indications of the route to London, and its condition. There is also action in Southwark, close to our London walk, where one of the hired thugs is hit on the head by a falling shop blind. Many authors have been inspired by particular places and the surrounding landscape. A good book will often leave the reader with a desire to visit the location. On the other hand, the landscape detective will enjoy a book like *Lark Rise to Candleford* even more if he has prospected the area beforehand.

Food

The walks were not chosen for their culinary delights, but both authors are fond of their food and enjoyed sampling regional dishes. It is remarkable, in fact, how in such a small area as the British Isles so many regional dishes abound. We had pie and peas in Yorkshire, venison and superb salmon caught locally in Tayside, as well as Loch Fyne kippers. It all adds to the enjoyment of the walk – but it also does rather more. Food has a message to tell about local conditions as well. The Yorkshire pie shop thrived in the days when whole families worked in the woollen mills and collected their hot pies on the way home. The Cornish pasty has its origins in the tin and copper mines, for miners do not come back to the surface for lunch. The pasty had to be a meal in itself – meat and two veg in a pastry case. The Loch Fyne kipper reminded us of the importance of the herring fleet in the history of Scotland. Scotland makes one think of porridge for breakfast. This is made from oatmeal, so you might expect Scotland grain mills processing oats to be rather different from English flour mills. And so it proves, for the meal mill has a distinctive kiln attached for baking the oats.

Some months after the Walberswick walk we were given a strange vegetable to eat called samphire (the name is a corruption of Saint Peter, the fisherman). Bright green fronds lying on the plate looked rather like seaweed. It was marsh samphire, which grows in saltmarshes near the coast of Suffolk. A geological map marks samphire beds near Walberswick.

Once the landscape detective starts to look around, the habit forms quite quickly. A glimpse of a sign such as 'Mill Lane' or an uncharacteristic shape in the landscape has led the authors on many an unscheduled detour. More and more we come across pieces of the jigsaw that add to our knowledge of an area – perhaps a hard fact, a detail, a recollection, a theory, a picture, or an opinion. This book is intended as a manual to help the reader follow the clues. 'You know my methods, Watson,' said the great detective. 'Apply them.'

FURTHER READING

Series

Green, E. R. R. (ed.), *Industrial Archaeology of the British Isles* (David & Charles).

Hoskins, W. G., and Milward, Roy, *The Making of the English Landscape* (Hodder & Stoughton).

Pevsner, Nikolaus, *Buildings of England* (Penguin).

Victoria History of the Counties of England.

Individual Titles

Aston, Michael, and Bond, James, *The Landscape of Towns* (Dent, 1976).

Beresford, Maurice, *The Lost Villages of England* (Alan Sutton, 1983).

Brunskill, R. W., *Illustrated Handbook of Vernacular Architecture* (Faber, 1971).

Burton, Anthony, *The National Trust Guide to Our Industrial Past* (George Philip, 1983).

Clayton, Peter, *Archaeological Sites of Great Britain*, 2nd edn (Batsford, 1985).

Clifton-Taylor, Alec, *The Pattern of English Building* (Faber, 1972).

Hoskins, W. G., *Fieldwork in Local History*, 2nd edn (Faber, 1982).

Hoskins, W. G., *The Making of the English Landscape*, 2nd edn (Hodder & Stoughton, 1977).

Muir, Richard, *Shell Guide to Reading the Landscape* (Michael Joseph, 1981).

Pugh, R. B. (ed.), *Victoria History of the Counties of England, General Introduction* (Oxford University Press, 1970).

Rackham, Oliver, *Trees and Woodland in the British Landscape* (Dent, 1976).

Ransom, P. J. G., *The Archaeology of Railways* (World's Work, 1981).

Richardson, John, *The Local Historian's Encyclopaedia* (Historical Publications, 1974).

Riden, Philip, *Local History* (Batsford, 1983).

Rolt, L. T. C., *Navigable Waterways* (Longman, 1969).

Rowley, Trevor, *Villages in the Landscape* (Dent, 1978).

Smith, J. T., and Yates, E. M., *On the Dating of English Houses from External Evidence* (Classey, 1972).

Taylor, Christopher, *Fields in the English Landscape* (Dent, 1975).

Taylor, Christopher, *Roads and Tracks of Britain* (Dent, 1979).

Whittow, J. B., *Geology and Scenery in Scotland* (Pelican, 1977).

Wignall, C. J., *Complete British Railways Maps and Gazetteer* (ORPC, 1983).

INDEX